The Blue Max Airmen
German Airmen Awarded the Pour le Mérite
Volume 15

Udet

Lance J. Bronnenkant, PhD

The Blue Max Airmen
German Airmen Awarded the Pour le Mérite
Volume 15
Udet
Lance J. Bronnenkant, PhD

I would like to thank the following colleagues, who were generous in their contributions to this work: The 1914–1918 Aviation Heritage Trust, Rainer Absmeier, Dick Bennett, Christophe Cony, Jean Devaux, Charles Gosse, Jack Herris, Jörn Leckscheid, David Méchin, Colin Owers, Bob Pearson, Bruno Schmäling, Josef Scott, Alan Toelle, Adam Wait, Aaron Weaver, and Reinhard Zankl.

And my special thanks go to my highly respected colleague and good friend, Greg VanWyngarden, whose generous sharing of his vast knowledge of Udet and his aircraft made this volume so much better than it otherwise would have been.

Interested in WWI aviation? Join The League of WWI Aviation Historians (**www.overthefront.com**), Cross & Cockade International (**www.crossandcockade.com**), and Das Propellerblatt (**www.propellerblatt.de**)

Text © 2020 Lance J. Bronnenkant, PhD.
Design and layout: Jack Herris
Cover design: Aaron Weaver
Aircraft Colors and Markings: Greg VanWyngarden
Color Profiles: Bob Pearson
Digital photo editing: Lance Bronnenkant & Jack Herris

Publisher's Cataloging-in-Publication data
Bronnenkant, Lance J.
 The Blue Max Airmen: German Aviators Awarded the Pour le Mérite: Volume 15 / by Lance J. Bronnenkant.
 p. cm.
 ISBN 978-1-953201-11-9
1. Udet, Ernst, 1896–1941. 2. World War, 1914–1918 --Aerial operations, German. 3. Fighter pilots -- Germany. 8. Aeronautics, Military --Germany -- History. II. Title.
ND237 .S6322 2011
759.13 --dc22   2011904920

Aeronaut Books

Books for Enthusiasts by Enthusiasts
www.aeronautbooks.com

Table of Contents

Ernst Udet

Above: *Lt.* Ernst Udet had this and other portraits taken of him at A. Buck's studio in Munich while he was on leave there in April-May 1918. He is wearing the *Pour le Mérite* that had been delivered to him by a Berlin jeweler around mid-May. The *Feldschnalle* (ribbons' bar) on his chest displays the ribbons for his (left to right): Iron Cross, 2nd Class; Royal Hohenzollern House Order, Knight's Cross with Swords; Württemberg's Merit Cross with Swords. His Iron Cross, 1st Class and Pilot's Badge are pinned to his tunic below his *Feldschnalle*.

Ernst Udet – The Man

Introduction

Most World War I aviation enthusiasts are familiar with Ernst Udet's 1935 autobiography, *Mein Fliegerleben* (*My Airman's Life*) or its British and American translations respectively titled *Ace of the Black Cross* (1937) and *Ace of the Iron Cross* (1970). Lesser known, however, is Udet's original memoir, *Kreuz wider Kokarde* (*Cross versus Cockade*), published in 1918. Independent sources have demonstrated that the dates and details of many of the events presented in *Mein Fliegerleben* and *Kreuz wider Kokarde* are generally more accurate and reliable than comparable works by other World War I aviators. What follows then makes extensive use of these autobiographical sources – particularly the rare *Kreuz wider Kokarde* which has not been translated into English – for Udet's story up through the end of World War I. In addition, Armand van Ishoven's biography, *Udet* (1977), presented in English as *The Fall of an Eagle: The Life of Fighter Ace Ernst Udet* (1979), is the primary source for Udet's post-war life.

Youth and Early Military Career

Ernst Udet, the only son of Adolf and Paula (née Krüger) Udet, was born in Frankfurt am Main on 26 April 1896. Adolf, a successful engineer, moved the family to Munich soon afterwards and it was in that city's Theresien-Gymnasium that Ernst received his formal education. His interest in aviation came early, as demonstrated by the "Aero-Club München 1909" that he, Otto Bergen, and Willy Götz formed that year. They hung around the Gustav Otto Flugmaschinenwerke (Gustav Otto Flying Machine Works) and built models based on what they saw as well as their own instincts. Udet's fascination with flight interfered with his education and led to an early disappointment, however, as Udet wryly observed:

"In the Gymnasium, my interest in aviation resulted in my teachers predicting the worst for my future. Anyway, I was 'allowed' to repeat a class – the initial outcome of my study of flight. After some time I built an airplane model that I wanted to let fly over the Isar [River]. Everything was well prepared and the compressed air motor pumped full; so I handed the model over to the element for which it was intended – the air. But after a few moments it became intimate with another element which it should have had nothing to do with: it fell into the water along with all of my hopes."[1]

Udet subsequently worked at his father's boiler factory and was taught welding. He then spent time in France at Luc-sur-Mer and Verdun learning French and teaching German to fellow students before returning to Munich. His interest in aviation had not diminished, however, and he finally went up for the first time in an airplane with Leo Roth from the Gustav Otto Flying Machine Works in 1913. He also passed his high school examination that year and

Above: Udet, Otto Bergen, and Willy Götz, founding members of the "Aero-Club München 1909," gather together at the fence bordering the Gustav Otto Flying Machine Works.

was rewarded with the gift of a motorcycle by his father.

When the war broke out in August 1914, the diminutive Udet – who reached a height of only 160 cm. (5 ft. 3 in.) as an adult – tried to enter military service but was rejected: "I was only 18 years old and not so well developed physically that I could count on being admitted to any military unit."[2] Still, the army was looking for civilian volunteers to act as couriers and he had his own motorcycle. "I immediately registered myself as a gentleman motorcyclist [i.e., an owner/driver as opposed to a chauffeur] with the Allgemeine Deutsche Automobil Klub, which was acting as the middleman for the Army."[3] Udet, "dressed in a heavy leather suit and provided with military headgear," left Munich on 18 August and arrived in Strasbourg two days later. From there, he linked up with his assigned unit, Württemberg's *26. Reserve-Division*, at Schirmeck.

"We received a pistol as an extra weapon and in this way became soldiers in the twinkling of an eye; but exactly how we were to be used was not very clear. For the most part, our activity was initially restricted to the post office. Military despatch riders were preferred for more important assignments."[4]

As time progressed and the unit advanced through Rothau and Saales to Saint-Dié-des-Vosges, the war had more serious implications for Udet. He noted, for example, that one rider was killed and another committed suicide following a nervous breakdown. He himself had a narrow escape when he was forced to flee from the French shelling of Saint-Dié-des-Vosges and ended up smashing his motorcycle in a shell hole. Forced to return to Strasbourg for motorcycle repairs, he discovered upon their completion that the *26. Reserve-Division* had been transferred to Belgium. He rode by train and then

Left: Udet astride the motorcycle that his father gifted him after he had passed his high school examinations.

motorcycle to Namur, where he was informed that no one knew where the division had gone, but that he was welcome to stay at the *Kraftwagenpark* (Motor Vehicle Depot) in town. He did so for one month and during that time got to know some of the aviation officers stationed nearby:

"One time I was even allowed to join a flight as an observer. That awakened my enthusiasm for flying again. That is why I tried to get into a *Flieger-Abteilung* in Belgium – unfortunately without success. When the voluntary motorcyclists' contracts came to an end, I returned home with the firm intention of reporting to a *Flieger-Ersatz-*

Abteilung. Despite recommendations, however, it was not easy to get into one quickly. At that time, there was quite a rush on the *FEAs*; particularly numerous were the active officers and NCOs who had precedence. I would have had to wait for months before being accepted."[5]

So Udet figured that he could shorten that period by obtaining a civilian pilot's license at Gustav Otto's aircraft factory. "My father paid 2,000 Marks and furnished a bathroom for Mr. Otto" in return for flying lessons, which began in February 1915 and ended in late April when he was awarded his license.[6] "And so I turned ever so hopefully to *Flieger-*

Abteilung Darmstadt and – twice sewn holds better – to Döberitz as well."[7] He also sent an application to a *Flieger-Ersatz-Abteilung* (*FEA*) at Warnemünde.

FEA 9 at Darmstadt was the first to accept him on 15 June 1915 and he reported there to begin his military flight training as a *Flieger* (private); however, the *Vizefeldwebel* leader of the company he had been assigned to would not permit Udet to attend the flight school. Despite various attempts by Udet to persuade his "*Vize*" that he had been accepted at the school due to his civilian license, the man would not budge. So Udet went over his head to the school CO, *Hptm.* Bruno Steffen, who had him flying an old LVG the same evening. Udet completed all three tests required to earn the Army Pilot's Badge and was subsequently assigned to a frontline unit, *Artillerie-Flieger-Abteilung* (*AFA*) 206 at Heiligkreuz (today's Sainte-Croix-en-Plaine), on 4 September 1915.[8]

Two-Seater Pilot

Udet told the following story regarding his new posting. *Lt.* Bruno Justinus was at Darmstadt searching for pilots to join his unit, *AFA* 206, which had recently been formed on 6 August.[9] One day, he sent for Udet and interrogated him about his qualifications and youth. Evidently liking what he heard, he asked Udet to be his pilot on the spot. Udet accepted of course, and the pair went out on the town to celebrate their "marriage" as "Emil and Franz" – the respective nicknames for a pilot and observer team. When confronted with the fact that Udet had stayed out beyond the time permitted on his pass, Justinus simply draped his officer's cape over Udet's shoulders and shuttled him past the sentries.[10]

On 14 September, Justinus and Udet were ordered to participate in a mission to bomb Belfort. It was only their second time together over enemy territory and it almost became their last. Unable to see their target because of thick cloud cover, they were just turning back when a loud twang sounded and the aircraft began to spin toward the ground. A shackle anchoring a guy wire in the upper right wing had broken. Udet, pressing the right rudder bar and turning the steering wheel with all his might, managed to pull out of the spin but had to throttle back to keep the airplane from going into another. Although they could glide down to the ground in this manner, when they emerged from the clouds over Montbéliard, they realized that they were far away from friendly territory. So they headed toward Switzerland to the east. Udet tried applying more throttle to gain altitude, but the airplane threatened to spin again and he had to power down a second time. Then:

Above: Udet when he was a volunteer motorcyclist for the military in 1914.

"Justinus stands up, slowly climbs out of his observer cockpit – my heart beat in my throat watching him – onto the right wing, feeling his way to the center strut. There he lets himself down, his legs dangling in the air. We are 1,600 meters high. I give it gas again, and the machine tips to the side. The counterbalance provided by Justinus is noticeable, but it is too little."[11]

Udet's arms started to cramp from the strain of holding the wheel and threatened to fail him. After signaling Justinus to return to his cockpit:

"A couple of powerful blows make the machine shake, the thin wooden wall of the observer's cockpit splinters, two hands appear – two bleeding hands scraped by splintered wood – grope around in the air and grab hold of the steering wheel. Justinus

Above & Right: The debris of Udet's first victory, a Farman MF 11 from *Escadrille MF* 29, somewhere at the outskirts of Mulhouse, with one of the crewmen still trapped in the wreck. Under magnification, we can see that the dead man's crash helmet was the one that Udet wore in several photographs and described in *Mein Fliegerleben* (opposite p.49) as: "*Bequem war er nicht, praktisch auch nicht…aber selbst erbeutet!*" ("It wasn't comfortable, it wasn't practical… but I'd captured it myself!")

is there, Justinus is helping me!"[12]

The ploy bought them more time and they crossed the Swiss border near Saint-Dizier. Udet alternately applied and reduced power as Justinus shouted to him to keep on going to Germany. They passed over Courtemaîche and Vendlincourt, Switzerland before landing in an open field just inside the German border: "There is no more *Leutnant* Justinus and *Flieger* Udet, only "Franz" and "Emil," two kids hopping about like Sioux Indians dancing around a stake, picking up clods of dirt and throwing them at each other as though they were snowballs."[13]

Ten days later on 24 September, Justinus was awarded the Iron Cross, 1st Class and Udet its 2nd Class for their remarkable effort in returning their damaged Aviatik B.II to Germany. Udet's promotion

to *Gefreiter* on 21 September was probably attributable to this effort as well.

Within days of their awards, Udet and Justinus took off on another bombing mission. When Udet made a sharp turn over their airfield, their airplane, burdened with a full fuel supply, bombs, and the addition of a machine gun, lost airspeed and sideslipped to earth. In his 1918 book, Udet briefly summarized:

"A slight fracture of the kneecap, dizziness, and a transfer from the *Abteilung* to the *Flugpark* [*Armee-Flug-Park* (*AFP*) Gaede] were the consequences of this event. I spent 10 days in the hospital and had

Above: Members of the newly-formed *Jasta* 15 pose in October 1916 at Habsheim with their comrades from *FFA* 48. From left to right: *Offz-Stv.* Karl Weingärtner (*Jasta* 15), *Lt.* Hellmuth Wendel (15), *Vzfw.* Ernst Udet (15), *Vzfw.* Willy Glinkermann (15), *Lt.* Hans-Olaf Esser (15), *Oblt.* Hermann Kropp (CO, *Jasta* 15), *Lt.* Kurt Haber (15), *Lt.* Grieben (*FFA* 48), *Oblt.* von Westarp (48), *Lt.* von Wedel (48), *Lt.* Willi Schulz (48), medical Dr. Drouven, *Lt.* Eberhard Hänisch (15), *Lt.* Kaufmann (48), *Lt.* von Freeden (48), *Lt.* Friedrich Weitz (15). (photo courtesy of Greg VanWyngarden)

time to think about the cause of my crash. I decided that in the future I would only do sharp turns at higher altitudes."[14]

What was not disclosed until his 1935 autobiography was that Udet also had to endure a week in a Neubreisach (today's Neuf-Brisach) stockade due to, as the CO of *AFP* Gaede had him repeat every day, his "careless, wild" turning over the airfield.[15] When he was about to report back to the *Park* to learn if he would ever be permitted to fly again, he was waylaid by *Leutnant* Hartmann, an observer who needed a pilot to take him on a bombing run that had just left. Udet eagerly volunteered and flew Hartmann to Belfort to drop his bombs. While doing so, however, one of the bombs became tangled in the undercarriage. Udet ironically thought :"'Banking and turning is forbidden!' How I wish that the CO of our *Flugpark* was sitting here at the wheel!" as he resorted to various maneuvers that ended with a steep bank to shake it loose.[16] Udet reported to the *Park*'s CO right after landing, and there, expecting

further punishment, was instead rewarded with a transfer to *Kampfeinsitzer-Kommando* (*KEK*) Habsheim – a single-seat fighter unit! It turns out that the *Stabsoffizier der Flieger* (Staff Officer for Aviation, or *Stofl*) at Mulhouse had telephoned to see if Udet had returned from arrest. When told that he had indeed returned but had then gone on a mission as soon as he had stepped foot on the airfield, the *Stofl* quickly decided that Udet had the makings of a good fighter pilot. He would not be proved wrong.

Fighter Pilot

Udet began to familiarize himself with rotary-engined monoplanes at the *AFP*. Just two days later, he was entrusted with a new Fokker *Eindecker* to take with him to *KEK* Habsheim. Upon takeoff, however, the airplane stubbornly veered to the right. Udet tried to correct this by pushing the stick to the left, but nothing happened and man and machine crashed into a hangar. A shaken but uninjured Udet found himself under investigation once again. This time he was cleared, however, when it was

Above & Below: Two views of Udet's second victim, Breguet-Michelin IV No.229, brought down on 12 October 1916. The second image demonstrates that it was featured on a Paul Hoffman & Co. series postcard. (first image courtesy of Greg VanWyngarden)

determined that the machine gun cable attached to the control stick had gotten tangled on a fuel feed switch, thus preventing any steering to the left.[17] The Park eventually supplied him with an older, used *Eindecker* to take with him to his new assignment.

Udet joined *Lt.* Otto Pfältzer (CO), *Uffz.* Karl Weingärtner, and *Gefr.* Willy Glinkermann at *KEK* Habsheim on 29 November 1915, the day after his promotion to *Unteroffizier*. His first combat as a fighter pilot occurred in December when he encountered a lone Caudron on patrol and they both flew straight at each other. When his opponent came into range and the moment of truth arrived, Udet froze and could not fire his machine gun. The Caudron's observer did not hesitate, however, and fired off a volley as he passed by the *Eindecker*, shooting off Udet's goggles and sending glass splinters into his face. Udet, bewildered at his lack of action and greatly ashamed, vowed that it would never happen again.[18] His second combat ended after his machine gun jammed, but his third – on 18 March 1916 – resulted in his first air victory. That afternoon, two French aircraft were reported as having crossed the lines heading northeast toward Altkirch. Udet, now a *Vizefeldwebel* as of 13 March, went up in a Fokker *Eindecker* to intercept them. When he did he was shocked to discover a formation of not two, but 23 total aircraft: 17 Farmans, three Caudrons, and three Breguet-Michelins that were on their way to bomb targets at Mulhouse. As they approached the city, Udet remembered his vow despite his being overwhelmingly outnumbered. He dove on a Farman in the middle of the formation and shot it down, causing it to crash in the city's outskirts. He was then joined by his three *KEK* Habsheim comrades who each claimed a victory as well. Although *Escadrille MF 29* indeed lost four aircraft that day, Udet's, Glinkermann's, and Weingärtner's claims were upheld whereas Pfältzer's was not.[19] Udet recalled in 1918 that his victim's crew consisted of a "*Kapitän und ein Unteroffizier*" ("captain and an NCO"). This confirms that the Farman MF 11 manned by *Capt.* Emile Bacon and *MdL.* Edouard Leroy was his first victory, for which he was awarded the Iron Cross, 1st Class two days later.[20]

If the chronology presented in *Kreuz wider Kokarde* is correct, sometime soon after this Udet had a narrow escape. He was coming back from a patrol in his *Eindecker* when the engine suddenly stopped. He knew he had to land soon and selected what he believed to be a pleasant meadow for his touchdown; however, as he got lower and nearer, the "meadow" turned out to be a tall cornfield. He

Above: A portrait of *Vzfw.* Ernst Udet. (photo courtesy of Greg VanWyngarden)

added: "To make matters worse, in the middle of the field was a dam which was almost a meter high and with which I soon became acquainted."[21] He heard a tremendous noise, and when his head cleared, discovered that he was trapped in the fuselage that had flipped over and dug itself into the ground. He too was upside down and his right knee had pushed through the side fabric, so he was unable to extricate himself unless he dug "through the earth like a mole." After about 15 minutes, all the while fearing that the airplane would catch on fire, he heard someone say in Alsatian German: "I can't find him. He must be dead." Then came the familiar voice of *Leutnant* Sigwarth – a comrade from a *KEK* that was based near the crash site. They all shouted to one another and a group of strong soldiers lifted the fuselage, freeing Udet. Although the *Eindecker* had lost both wings and its tail surface, and both the motor and machine gun had broken free of their mounts, Udet escaped injury.

Left: Udet and his close friend, *Offz-Stv.* Willy Glinkermann, attend to a pet. (photo courtesy of Greg VanWyngarden)

Jagdstaffel Pilot

After telling the story of his first victory, *Kreuz wider Kokarde* skips ahead to the events surrounding his second confirmed victory on 12 October 1916.[22] The chapter's opening paragraph, however, contains one of the comparatively few factual errors encountered in his works: "In the meantime, I had gotten a new Fokker biplane and belonged to a *Jagdstaffel* established on 10 September 1917." We know that Udet's new unit, *Jagdstaffel* 15, was officially created on 28 September 1916, became operational on 9 October, and was initially provided with Fokker D.II and D.III biplanes as well as personnel from *FFA* 48, *FFA* 68, and *KEK* Habsheim.[23]

Why the "10 September 1917" date was so far off and whether the mistake was attributable to Udet or his publisher remain unknown. At any rate, the chapter goes on to describe the events of 12 October 1916:

"About 20 kilometers behind our front, I observed a formation of seven Breguet biplanes flying toward the Rhine; they were protected by two Nieuports. When they flew directly under me, I had an easy job of it. I innocently got behind the lead airplane and forced it to land after 350 shots. Since it had landed safely and I wanted to prevent the airplane's destruction by its inhabitants, I landed next to it. As a result of a hit to one of my tires, I lightly overturned. It was a comical scene: the defeated safely landed and the victor with wheels up. The two Frenchmen climbed down from their framework and

we shook hands with one another. The pilot was a stocky little man who had been a detective in Nancy before the war. He told me that he actually was an acceptance pilot for a factory and had joined in this flight just for fun. The observer had been shot in the left arm and therefore spoke very little. The downed Breguet biplane had about 80 hits, which I noted with satisfaction. It still carried 30 bombs and at the front of the craft bore the proud inscription: '*Le voilà le foudroyant.*' ('Here comes the thunderbolt!')"[24]

The Breguet's captured crewmen were *Escadrille BM* 120's *Cpl.* René Bouet and his wounded observer, *Sol.* Marcel Delcroix. Many photographs were taken of Udet's trophy, including the ones seen on page 10 above.

Shortly after this second success, Udet was made a *Fähnrich*, or officer-candidate, on 17 October. This appears to have been a formality that led to his promotion to *Offizier-Stellvertreter*, or Warrant Officer, a few weeks later on 5 November. This sent him on the path to becoming a *Leutnant der Reserve* (2nd Lieutenant in the Reserves) – quite an achievement for someone who had first entered the military as a private just 17 months earlier. He was also recognized with Württemberg's Merit Cross with Swords on 4 November. Evidently, the Kingdom felt that Udet had been protecting its borders when he shot down the Breguet near Rustenhart.[25]

"*Der Dritte*" ("The Third") was the title of the next chapter in *Kreuz wider Kokarde* and was dedicated to

Right: Udet poses in front of a Fokker *Eindecker* at Habsheim airfield in September 1916. (photo courtesy of Greg VanWyngarden)

Udet's third victory, achieved on 24 December 1916.

"I was at the front when I saw two Caudrons, accompanied by a Nieuport single-seater, doing rangefinding for their artillery in the Niederaspach region. The two Caudrons circled over their sector, confident that they would be covered by the fighter airplane. I placed the sun at my back and flew at the opponents who were at the same altitude. One enemy reconnaissance plane approached me to within 200 meters, made a slow turn, and innocently flew right in front of me – certain evidence that the enemy had not seen me due to the strong glare of the sun. I moved in closer and could see the observer leaning far over the cockpit looking down. At that same instant I opened fire and the opponent's right motor began to burn. But this did not seem to bother the pilot, as he began to turn like a wildman, sometimes right, sometimes left.

Above: A *Jasta* 15 portrait taken at Habsheim on 15 October 1916. Left to right: *Offz-Stv.* Karl Weingärtner, *Lt.* Otto Pfältzer, *Lt.* Kurt Haber, *Lt.* Friedrich Weitz, *Lt.* Hellmuth Wendel, *Vzfw.* Heinrich Wendel, *Vzfw.* Ernst Udet.

After half a minute, however, the fire came thick and fast over the nacelle and the other motor and the opponent went down. At the point of impact, which was immediately behind the first enemy trench, one could still see the opponent's wreck burning and smoking 30 minutes later. The other reconnaissance plane got so frightened by the whole business that he dashed headlong for home while the fighter dove at me from above, started to fire from hundreds of meters away, but did not engage in closer combat."[26]

Udet's hapless victims were *Escadrille C 34's MdL*. Jean Hourcade and *Sous-Lt.* Louis Lombart in a Caudron G4. They fell within their own lines near Aspach-le-Haut (its German name was Oberaspach). With three confirmed successes to his credit, Udet was granted his officer's patent as a *Leutnant der Reserve* on 22 January 1917.

Kreuz wider Kokarde's next chapter was called *"Der gute Nieuport-Flieger"* ("The Good Nieuport Flier"), and although it did not specify a victory number, it appears to have concerned Udet's fourth, felled on 20 February 1917. First, Udet refers to flying a "brand new Albatros D.III" and that type was essentially introduced to the front in January

1917 (only 13 were present at the close of 1916). Second, Udet mentions that his opponent was in a "new Nieuport type" which could have meant the Nieuport 17bis that came out in late 1916 (it was noticeably different from the Nieuport 17 in that its fuselage sides were not flat but instead bulged outward from a series of horizontal stringers). Third, Udet says that the action took place over "A." and his fourth was brought down near Aspach. Last, we have Udet's description of the fight itself:

"He flew quite well and demonstrated all kinds of silly tricks for us, such as loops, lateral somersaults, vertical zooms, and the like. At 3,000 meters altitude – we had come a bit closer to the front in the meantime – I managed to riddle his motor. His propeller stopped. I then flew close up to him and saw how the cheeky guy lifted his gloved hand and threatened me. I did the same thing, but it did not seem to make an impression on him because he still tried to glide over his own lines. He nearly succeeded. Over A., we were only 400 meters up and it was high time that the fellow came down. My machine guns malfunctioned and I repeatedly flew right by him in order to force him to suddenly

Above: As the sign behind him proclaimed, Udet – now an *Offizier-Stellvertreter* as of 5 November 1916– could serve as the unit's *Offizier vom Dienst* (Duty Officer). He was raised to full officer status as a *Leutnant der Reserve* on 22 January 1917.

go down deeper to evade gusts and the like. He set down safely on a small field between the two foremost lines. The plane had not finished rolling when I saw a guy jump out of it and hop in great bounds toward the enemy barbed wire. In half a minute he disappeared into the enemy trenches. The airplane, a new Nieuport type, was shot on fire by our artillery a little later and then recovered by our night patrol."[27]

A Nieuport from *Escadrille N* 81 made a forced landing near Aspach that day after having been shot up in combat. Its pilot, *MdL.* Pierre de Casenove de Pradines, escaped unscathed and returned to duty. Air historian Jon Guttman interviewed de Casenove de Pradines in 1978, who said:

"It is true that I was hit in the motor at 300 meters and my machine gun stopped or jammed. I glided into the frontlines, despite the ground fire, to find a landing site. I had just landed in No Man's Land when I was off and running to get back to the French

trenches, which seemed a long way off, sprinting from shell hole to shell hole."[28]

De Casenove de Pradines denied ever having shaken his fist at Udet, however.

Jasta 15 moved its airfield from Habsheim to La Selve (Aisne) on 5 March 1917. Udet wrote:

"My first victory on this front occurs on 24 April. I meet a Nieuport over Chavignon, shoot him down in flames after a short dogfight, and see his remains smashed to pieces in the crater field. It is my fifth confirmed victory..."[29]

Despite his description of what surely would have been a kill, no suitable candidate for his victim has been discovered to date. The same is true for his sixth, which was a SPAD VII said to have fallen near "Bois de Ville" on 5 May. By this time, the unit had been moved to an airfield outside of Boncourt. Although no "Bois de Ville" can be found within what were *Jasta* 15's hunting grounds at the time,

just 20 kilometers south of Boncourt is La Ville-aux-Bois-lès-Pontavert – the probable location referred to by Udet.[30] Some historians have offered that Udet's victim may have been *Escadrille N 3*'s *Capt.* Alfred Heurtaux, who was wounded in action that day in a SPAD VII but managed to make it back to his base near the La Bonne Maison farm, just to the south of

Fismes. However, *Esc. N* 3's original log book notes that Heurtaux was wounded between 7:00 and 7:30 a.m. whereas Udet's claim was at 5:30 p.m.[31]

Death and Chivalry

Lt. Heinrich Gontermann had been placed in charge of *Jasta* 15 following the death of its second CO,

Oblt. Max Reinhold, on 26 April. Shortly after his arrival on 2 May, Gontermann garnered his 18th victory the day before Udet's sixth. By 11 May, he had amassed 21 victories and was thereby qualified for the *Pour le Mérite*, which he received on 15 May. When he was sent on four weeks of leave as part of his reward, Udet was placed in temporary command of the unit.[32] During Gontermann's absence, *Jasta* 15 suffered heavy losses that included Udet's close friends and colleagues, *Lt.* Eberhard "Puz" Hänisch, *Vzfw.* Willy "Glinkerle" Glinkermann, and *Vzfw.* Wilhelm Eichenaur.[33] Udet was so badly affected that on 4 June – the day of Eichenaur's death – he wrote another friend, *Oblt.* Kurt Grasshoff (formerly with *Jasta* 15) who was now in charge of *Jasta* 37:

"I want to go to another front. I would like to come to you. I'm the last of *Jasta* 15, the last of those who once left Muelhausen to go to the Champagne."[34]

While awaiting Grasshoff's response, Udet says that he experienced one of the more famous examples of chivalry in the air when he came up against none other than *Esc. N 3*'s *Capt.* Georges Guynemer, France's *as des as* (ace of aces) at the time with 45 victories. In 1935's *Mein Fliegerleben*, Udet stated that while he was temporarily in charge of *Jasta* 15, he decided to go after a captive balloon. After he had flown to a great height from which to attack the balloon:

"A small dot is rapidly approaching from the west.

Unser erfolgr. Kampfflieger
Leutnant Udet
Führer einer Jagdstaffel.

604
Postkartenvertrieb W. Sanke
BERLIN N. 37.
Nachdruck wird gerichtlich verfolgt.

Left: Udet stands in front of a hangar housing Albatros fighters, time and place unknown. This was his first appearance in Willi Sanke's airmen postcard series but it would not be his last. He was featured on four more Sanke cards before the war ended.

Above: Members of *Jasta* 37 celebrate Udet's award of the Royal Hohenzollern House Order, Knight's Cross with Swords, granted to him on 13 November 1917.

Small and black at first, it grows quickly as it approaches. A SPAD, an enemy combat pilot. A loner like me, up here, on the prowl. I straighten up in my seat. There's going to be a fight. We go for each other at the same height, whizzing by each other at a hair's breadth. We bank into a left turn. The other's apparatus shines light brown in the sun. Then the circling begins. From below, it might appear as though two large birds of prey were courting one another, but up here it's a game of death…Sometimes we race so close together that I can clearly see a slender, pale face under the leather helmet. There is a word in black letters on the fuselage, between the wings. As he passes me for the fifth time, so close that his propeller wash shakes me back and forth, I can make it out: *"Vieux"* it says there – *vieux* – the old one. That's Guynemer's sign.[35]…I do a half loop in order to come down on him from above. He catches on at once and also starts to loop. I try a turn, and Guynemer follows me. Once, coming out of a turn, he latches onto me for a few seconds. Metallic hailstones rattle through my right wing and ring out lightly as they strike

the struts. I try everything I can, the tightest banks, turns, side slips, but he anticipates all my moves with lightning speed and immediately reacts to each one with lightning speed. Gradually, I realize he is superior to me. Not only is the machine over there better, but the man in it can do more than me. But I keep fighting. Another turn. For a moment he comes into my sights. I push the button on the stick…the machine gun is silent…a gun jam! With my left hand clutching the stick, my right attempts to reload [the gun]. No use – the stoppage remains. For a moment I think of diving away. But that would be useless with such an opponent – he would immediately be on my neck and shoot me to pieces. We continue to twist and turn. Beautiful flying if the stakes weren't so high. I have never had such a tactically clever opponent…For eight minutes we we are twisting around each other – it is the longest eight minutes of my life. Now, lying on his back, he races over me. I let go of the stick for a moment and hammer the machine gun with both fists…Guynemer observed this motion from above, he must have seen it, and now he knows what is up with me. He knows that

Above & Below: Udet (far left) strikes a comical pose with other members of *Jasta* 37 in the first image. Note the box that he was standing on to raise himself up closer to their head level. Left to right: Udet, *Lt.* Ascan Klee-Gobert, *Lt.* Krämer, *Lt.* Karl Haustein, unknown, *Lt.* Bitterscha, *Vzfw.* Falke, *Lt.* Heinrich Zempel, *Fw.* Walter Horn, *Vzfw.* Bärwald. Second image, taken at the same time (left to right): Krämer, Zempel, Klee-Gobert, Haustein, Udet, unknown, Falke, Bitterscha, Horn, Bärwald. (second image courtesy of Bruno Schmäling)

Facing Page: A rarely-seen portrait of Udet. The second ribbon on his ribbon bar represented the Royal Hohenzollern House Order, Knight's Cross with Swords that he was awarded on 13 November 1917. The first and third ribbons were for the Iron Cross, 2nd Class and Württemberg's Merit Cross with Swords that he had earned beforehand. (photo courtesy of Greg VanWyngarden)

I'm his helpless prey. He sweeps over me again, almost on his back. That is when it happened: he sticks out his hand and waves to me, waves lightly, and dives down to the west, heading for his front. I fly home, dazed. There are people who say that Guynemer had a gun jam himself back then. Others claim he feared I might ram him in despair. But I don't believe them. I still believe to this day that a bit of chivalry from the past continued to survive. And because of that, I lay this belated wreath on Guynemer's unknown grave."[36]

Udet never mentioned this particular incident in 1918's *Kreuz wider Kokarde*, but he did relate a very similar one. Again, he began by saying that while with *Jasta* 15, he decided to go after a balloon:

"From a great height, I went down at the balloon in a gliding flight. When I was still about 4,000 meters from it, I noticed a small point that got behind me and became increasingly larger. After a few seconds, it turned out to be a SPAD single-seater who had apparently waited for me to fly over the French front in order to finish me off. I was only at 1,600 meters' altitude and could no longer possibly engage in a dogfight since the fight would have been observed by enemy airmen, whereupon I would certainly have had to deal with superior numbers. So I turned toward the troublemaker and discovered that he flew quite skilfully and had a better airplane than I. We flew in circles so close to one another that I could see down into his cockpit. I constantly saw his white, gleaming face and a long, fluttering scarf. As a distinguishing mark, he carried a large, black *Totenkopf* [skull and crossbones symbol] on both sides of his fuselage. A clever maneuver got me into his sights and I received several hits to the fuselage just behind my seat and one hit to my backrest's padding that grazed my flight suit. It was high time for me to beat it, and I spun down about 500 meters, righted myself, and pressed for our lines. My opponent was quite decent because even though he followed me down, he no longer attacked but only accompanied me to the front and then flew home."[37]

The similarities between these accounts are striking and one has to wonder if the one published in 1918 was the basis for the more embellished one presented in 1935. It should be noted that by the time the Guynemer story appeared in *Mein Fliegerleben*, the tale of a pilot letting his opponent go 'with a wave' when he realized his guns had jammed had already become well-established in the 'knightly' lore of World War I air combat. For example, in the 30 October 1919 edition of *Flight* magazine, it was related that while visiting with Lothar von Richthofen in February 1918, Austro-Hungarian diplomat Count Otto von Czernin was informed that during a circling fight, "suddenly something jammed in Richthofen's machine gun, and he could not fire any more. The Englishman looked wonderingly across, and when he realized what the matter was with Richthofen he waved his hand, turned around and flew off."[38] Even the 1927 silent movie *Wings* had its American hero suffering a gun jam, hammering at his weapon to clear it, being observed doing so by his German pursuer, who then gallantly waved to him and flew off. It is also the case that historian Jean-Marc Binot, in his 2017 study of Georges Guynemer, could find no evidence of such an encounter – particularly in June 1917 – in *Spa* 3 records, and argued that compared to other notations in the records, "if he had had an eight minute-long dogfight, as Udet claims in his book, the Frenchman would have mentioned it – if only in a single line." Moreover, based on his assessment of Guynemer as an ambitious, aggressive pilot who cared little for Germans, he concluded it was highly unlikely that Guynemer would have let Udet go. We also have the report that when Udet was interviewed by a French journalist during the Winter Olympics of 1936, he spoke only of "an embryo of a combat" with Guynemer that Udet himself chose to break off and dive away from when his guns jammed – which sounds more like the *Kreuz wider Kokarde* version.[39] Accordingly, although we would like the Guynemer tale to have been true, there are reasons to suspect that the substitution of Guynemer for an unknown French pilot and the chivalrous release of an opponent after seeing that his guns had jammed were later embellishments. Even so, we can at least applaud Udet for generously portraying an erstwhile opponent in a positive and heroic light.

A Change of Venue

Gontermann returned from his leave on 19 June and when Udet informed him that he was requesting a transfer to *Jasta* 37, he promised that he would stay on long enough to break in replacements. True to his word, he did just that and only left for *Jasta* 37 via *AFP* 4 on 6 August 1917. Soon after his arrival at *Jasta* 37's airfield at Phalempin, he encountered his first English opponent:

"My first meeting with a representative of 'Old England' turned out to be quite pleasant. I was flying alone again, as usual, when I saw a formation of five Nieuport single-seaters pressing after several German Albatros aircraft in the region of Lens. One

Nieuport was going after an Albatros so doggedly that he apparently did not notice my approach. At about 3,000 meters' altitude, I got behind him and fired off a few shots in order to give my guns a quick test. This made such an impression on the Englishman that he immediately throttled up and rushed down head over heels. I had trouble keeping up with him and when he caught himself at about 400 meters' altitude to try to reach his front, I fired off a few more shots, whereupon he immediately went down to the German side to land. Since the [manifold] pressure on my airplane had dropped due to the dive and the engine would not get going properly, I decided to land next to the Englishman. I had hardly touched down when he came right over to me. He shook my hand and told me I was a 'real sportsman.' We smoked a good, perfumed English cigarette, and after he declared that there was nothing more to be done with his Nieuport, he went away under the protection of two 'field greys.' His airplane had been hit only once in the wing."[40]

This fairly detailed description has confounded historians because Udet was not credited with a Nieuport close to his arrival at *Jasta* 37. In fact, his next Nieuport victory did not occur until January 1918.[41] Moreover, the tales of his next two victims – his seventh and eighth – followed right after this account in his book, so the Nieuport incident preceded them and evidently was not awarded to him. So why was Udet denied a victory when the pilot and airplane were captured? And who would that pilot have been? Udet related that he shot down the airplane that would be counted as his seventh "the next day." His seventh fell on 14 August, so 13 August would seem to be the date for this Nieuport incident; however, no Nieuport or any other aircraft that would suit Udet's tale above was brought down on the 13th. A very close fit, however, can be found on 12 August. RFC No.40 Squadron's Nieuport 23 A6771.1 was brought down somewhere near Douai (in the region of Lens) and its pilot, 2Lt. W.D. Cullen, captured. Cullen's account after his repatriation related: "Patrol of five attacked 2 EAs but engine failed in dive, then chased down by two Albatros near Douai."[42] Udet failed to mention that another Albatros – flown by *Uffz.* Josef Heiligers of *Jasta* 30 – had also attacked Cullen; hence, Cullen's reference to "two Albatros." It turns out that Heiligers and Udet both put in a claim for Cullen's machine and that a court of arbitration awarded the victory to Heiligers.[43]

As mentioned above, Udet's seventh victory occurred on 14 August 1917. Of it, he wrote:

"At 8:00 p.m., five Bristol two-seaters flew over me in an easterly direction. Apparently, they were on a bombing mission. I stayed between them and the front and caught the returning opponents. I shot at the lead airplane directly from in front, flew under him, and found that the opponent was already beginning to smoke. Nevertheless, he turned the tables in a flash and quickly became the attacker. I came into his field of fire by too large a turn on my part. I dropped almost vertically to escape him again. After a fall of about 500 meters, I carefully caught myself again and noticed from new fire close up that my opponent was still right behind me. I repeated the same maneuver a second time. In the meantime, we had come down to 3,000 meters. The tension wires howled and I feared that the machine would break apart at any moment due to the tremendous demand being placed upon it. Suddenly, I heard a mighty bang behind me. I turned around and saw to my joy that the Englishman had exploded, either by overloading his engine or because I had previously holed his fuel tank or his engine casing. The observer and pilot, with limbs stretched wide, passed by me, then the engine, wheels, fuselage, etc…After this incident, I decided to be more cautious in the future and not underestimate the English as I had in the beginning."[44]

The aircraft was actually a DH.4 (similar in appearance to the Bristol F2.b) from No.25 Squadron, RFC.[45] In addition, *Jasta* 30's *Lt.* Heinrich Brügman had been attacking the airplane when it exploded, sending metal fragments into Brügman's Albatros. Brügman was not credited with the victory, however – perhaps because he was killed the next day in combat and was therefore unable to contest Udet's claim, or because Udet had already lost a claim to another *Jasta* 30 pilot the day before.

Udet's eighth followed the next day:

"I had just returned from a hunting flight when the mechanics suddenly shouted: 'An Englishman, an Englishman!' We all looked in the direction they pointed at and sure enough, barely 200 meters high, a Sopwith flew toward our field. I jumped into the closest machine, took off, armed only with goggles, still with a cold motor, just at the moment when the Englishman arrived at the edge of our field. Instead of making a run for it, the cheeky guy began to spray me with his machine gun. After a few turns, however, I got behind him and was able to fire at him from about 150 meters away. Meanwhile, reinforcements in the form of two aircraft from my *Staffel* were approaching, so the Tommy decided

ageb. Nr. *2280/18*

Jagdgruppe 3

J. Nr. *328/18* an u.ab 29.1.18

O. U., den 28. Januar 1918.

Leutnant u.stellv.Jagdgruppenfuehrer.

An

den Kommandeur der Flieger 4. Armee

durch Orolt. Jagdgruppe 3

[stamp: Armee-Oberkommando 4 / Kommandeur der Flieger / 31. JAN 1918 / A. Nr. 6964]

Mit der Bitte, die Anerkennung als ____ 18. ____ Sieg und ~~Verleihung des Ordens Pour le mérite an Leutnant Udet~~

Leutnant d.Res. U d e t

zu beantragen, wird nachstehende Abschussmeldung vorgelegt:

Datum: 28. Januar 18. Ort: nordw. Houthoulster Wald Zeit: 2. 30 nachm.

Flugzeugbesatzung: Fuehrer: Leutnant U d e t

Beobachter: _____

Typ, Nummer und Abzeichen der eigenen Maschine: Albatros D.V. 5368/17

Gefechtsbericht (Schilderung des Luftkampfes mit Angaben von Flughoehen, Schussentfernungen und besonderen beim Gegner bemerkten Abzeichen und Merkmalen):

In Gegend Klerken wurde meine Kette in ca. 4600m von mehreren S. E. 5 angegriffen. Ein S.E.5 mit Wimpeln am Schwanz stürzte sich hinter Vzf. Schulz her, wurde dann aber sofort von mir angegriffen und beschossen. Zunächst drückte ich ihn bis auf 900 m diesseits herunter. Dann richtete sich der Engländer etwas auf und flog stark drückend auf den Houthoulster-Wald zu, von mir beschossen. Als er so ein kurzes Stück geflogen war, fiel er plötzlich ziemlich steil ohne abzufangen im Trichter feld westlich des Houthoulster Waldes zu Boden.

[stamp: ...entum d... Reichsarch...]

Udet

Leutnant u. Staffelführer.

Wenden.

Above & Facing Page: Udet's request for confirmation of his victory on 28 January 1918. A translation of his description of the fight is given below on pages 36–37.

Zeugen: Lt. Haustein

         vzf. Schulz

Erdbeobachtung wegen starken Dunstes
nicht zu erhalten.

Bezug auf Anlage Nr. __1__

,,   ,,   ,,   Nr. __2__

,,   ,,   ,,   Nr. _____

,,   ,,   ,,   Nr. _____

,,   ,,   ,,   Nr. _____

Angaben ueber das abgeschossene Flugzeug:

     Liegt ~~diesseits~~/jenseits der Linien.

     Flugzeug-Typ: S. E. 5

     Flugzeug-Nr.

     Motorart:

     Motor-Nr.   nicht zu ermitteln, da jenseits.

     Pferdestaerke:

     Bewaffnung:

Flugzeugbesatzung:

     des Flugzeugfuehrers Dienstgrad:

   ,,   ,,   Name:

   ,,   ,,   Zugehoerigkeit:

     (Angabe ob tot, verwundet oder unverwundet gefangen):

     des Beobachters Dienstgrad:

   ,,   ,,   Name:

   ,,   ,,   Zugehoerigkeit:

     (Angabe wie vorher):

Besonderes im Flugzeug (Bomben, F.-T., Lichtbildgeraet usw.):

                                Leutnant u. Staffelführer.
                                Unterschrift des Abteilungsfuehrers.

to make himself scarce. A wild chase immediately started, quite suitable for the cinema. Initially, the opponent had tried to pull up into the clouds, which were about 300 meters up, in order to escape our field of fire. When this did not work out for him, however, he decided to withdraw in the opposite direction. He gunned it and went down to the ground. I was quite wrong about this tough fellow. Only now did the real fight begin. We tore off like crazy to the west at only 10 to 20 meters' altitude. If a village cropped up, we would spring over it with a bold hop. The business was not easy for me in this respect because due to the low flight, I did not dare to press right behind the opponent because I could easily sideslip from his strong prop wash and thereby unnecessarily endanger myself and my machine. Once he flew to the right side of an avenue and I to the left. During the course of this, his observer shot through the trees. We flew over a tethered balloon at very low altitude. Then the Tommy made a small turn and I fastened onto him from close behind. I shot at him for a long time until he began to smoke. Smoke is created when the fuel tank or engine casing is hit. The escaping fuel immediately evaporates after leaving the tank and forms a white cloud. It's a sure sign that the opponent will soon catch on fire. That was the case here, and just before he could land, bright flames erupted from the pilot's seat. The airplane overturned and exploded; the two occupants were incinerated."[46]

The crewmen, 2Lt. H.D.B. Snelgrove and 2AM W. Addison, had been flying in RFC No.43 Squadron's Sopwith Strutter A1079.B6. They had gotten as far as a spot between Harnes and Loison-sous-Lens.

Udet told the tale of his ninth which he brought down on 21 August 1917:

"In good weather, British bombing formations would usually fly through around 9:00 to 10:00 a.m. The Havilland two-seaters were mostly used for long distance bombing missions. So on this day, six Havillands flew over the front toward the east about five kilometers south of me. I immediately took up the chase alone, but soon discovered that catching up to the extremely fast opponents in my relatively slow Albatros airplane was unthinkable. I was able to keep a close eye on the increasingly fading opponents only with difficulty. Finding them was made even more difficult by the fact that flak fire stopped about 20 to 30 kilometers behind the front, so I only saw small dots that represented the aircraft. Finally, the Englishmen turned around over Valenciennes where they met up with a second English squadron consisting of six aircraft coming from the north. They now flew at 5,000 meters' altitude and I flew at approximately 4,900 meters. Both parties, as much as I could be called a party, flew toward one another. I came upon the lead airplane, which flew the lowest and at my altitude, in the neighborhood of Tournay. In order to stay as close as possible to him, I turned right in front of him, flew up behind him, and placed a decisive volley into his airplane from about 80 to 100 meters away. As the pilot later informed me, both fuel tanks and the motor were riddled by this volley, the observer killed by a head shot, and the pilot wounded by three shots. Smoking, the big beast slowly began its descent in front of me. I followed. I carefully kept on peeping at the empty observer place. I knew of cases where the observer had hidden within the bodywork, giving the impression that he had been hit; but then when the pursuing German airplane got well within his sights through a careless motion, he quickly got up, shot, and usually struck home. After following the opponent right under his tail for about 2,000 to 3,000 meters and firing repeatedly, I risked going a little above him and looked into the cockpit. I then ascertained that the observer had been hit and was lying in the fuselage. Meanwhile, the Englishman's propeller had stopped. Upon landing about 20 to 30 kilometers behind our lines, the airplane overturned and the dead observer was ejected in a large arc. The pilot slowly got out of his seat, crawled out, and sat down dejectedly near his companion's corpse. Later, I had the opportunity to speak with the one I'd shot down. He told tall tales about dogfights with several German single-seaters, etc. and thought himself to be terribly bold. He was a *Leutnant* and an Australian student."[47]

The airplane Udet had brought down near Ascq was DH.4 A7566 from No.55 Squadron, RFC. The unfortunate observer was 2Lt. J.L. Richardson, and his pilot, 2Lt. C.W. Davyes, was indeed from Australia. Presumably, Udet did not take much of a liking to Davyes because this episode was titled: *"Der australische Aufschneider"* ("The Australian Braggart"). The *Armeeoberkommando* (*AOK*) 6 report for the day confirms their identities: "*Am 21.8. vorm. bei Sainghin (südöstl. Lille) 1. engl. DD. (D.H.4) nach Luftkpf. abgesch. von J.S. 27. Beobachter Lt. Richardson tot, Führer Lt. Davis vers. im Kr.Laz. Milit. Hospital Lille; beide von der 55. sqn. IX. wing.*" ("On the morning of 21 August, 1 English biplane (DH.4) shot down after air combat by *Jagdstaffel* 27 near Sainghin[-en-Mélantois] (southeast of Lille). Observer Lt. Richardson dead, pilot Lt. Davis sent to war hospital Military Hospital Lille; both from No.55 Sqn., IX Wing.")

Above : Udet (left) suits up before a flight while he was the CO of *Jasta* 37. Note the British flight coat (which was actually a yellow-tan color that came out dark grey on the orthochrome film of the day) and British fur-lined cap. Several pilots prized such trophies and wore them on missions. This picture and U61 below in the Aircraft section were snapped at the same time.

Udet downed his 10th official victory on 17 September 1917. A photo of the airplane's wreckage – RFC No.41 Squadron's DH.5 A9409 – was included in *Kreuz wider Kokarde* (opposite page 65). In addition, a description of the fight, titled *"Ein Luftkampf mit De-Havilland Einsitzern"* ("A Dogfight with De Havilland Single-Seaters") appears in the work, although much later and out of sequence with his other victories. Udet had been partying the night before and was feeling somewhat under the weather:

"So I took off quickly before breakfast in order to bring my wellbeing back up to its best. I mechanically flew along the front toward the south. When I turned back around to the north again, I noticed German flak fire almost directly above me and right after that three English airplanes. I climbed to their altitude and watched them for a while. At first, I thought they were Sopwiths flying on their

Unser erfolgreicher Kampfflieger
Leutnant Udet

620
Postkartenvertrieb W. Sanke
BERLIN N. 37.
Nachdruck wird gerichtlich verfolgt.

phot. A. Buck, München

Left & Facing Page: Two more portraits (see page 4 above) taken at A. Buck's studio in Munich while Udet was on leave in April/May 1918. These two were featured on Sanke cards.

backs, because the upper wing – which is usually staggered forward on all English airplanes – was staggered backward in this case. 'It must be a brand new type,' I said to myself. The Englishmen tried everything possible with their new crates. They went into spins, made loops, did wingovers, and things like that. I was about 100 meters higher than them. When the first drew close to firing distance,

Unser erfolgreicher Kampfflieger
Leutnant Udet

621
Postkartenvertrieb W.Sanke
BERLIN N.32.
Nachdruck wird gerichtlich verfolgt.

phot. A. Buck, München

Right & Facing Page: Yet another two portraits (see pages 4 and 28–29 above) taken at A. Buck's studio in Munich while Udet was on leave in April/May 1918.

he pulled up and began to shoot. That brought me out of my repose somewhat. I turned my machine on its nose and fired too. All three thereupon moved off to the west and approached me again. This time, we were at the same altitude. The first flew at me from the front and began to shoot again. But when he saw that I certainly wasn't thinking of getting out of his way, he got scared at the last minute and turned about 30 meters in front of me, perhaps to get out of the way. I waited for this turn and got him dead in my sights. After a few well-aimed shots, his

new machine broke apart in the air while both of his comrades apparently lost their desire to fight. I went down behind the fallen opponent to ascertain the crash site. When I had circled over the place of impact, the two Tommies were excitedly circling around the same spot. I decided to attack them again after I had cleared the jam my machine guns had experienced during the [prior] attack. However, my plan was preempted by two German single-seat fighters that dove down on the two 'bunnies' from a great height. The second one came down in

Above & Facing Page: Two amusing images of *Jasta* 4 airmen interacting with some of their pets. In the first, a baboon is concentrating on unraveling *Lt.* Carlos Meyer-Baldó's cloth legging while a german shepherd watches. The three airmen to the left of Meyer-Baldó (left to right): *Lt.* Julius Bender, *Lt.* Johannes Jessen, Udet. In the second, the baboon has partly succeeded but has apparently taken exception to the german shepherd's attention. (photos courtesy of Greg VanWyngarden)

the meadow about 600 meters from my gentleman whereas the third was able to reach the English lines – but only with great difficulty."[48]

David B. Rogers, a writer for the *Toronto Star*, interviewed Udet in Berlin and published this "free translation" of Udet's combat report in 1931:

"At 7:30 a.m. while flying an Albatros D V 4476/17 at a height of approximately 8,500 feet, I sighted a British one-seater in the middle of a group of three enemy planes about one mile south of Izel. The sun was directly behind me. The enemy planes apparently did not see me at all. I attacked suddenly, holding my fire until within easy range. After almost the first burst, I saw that I had made a hit and that the plane was out of control. A moment later he crashed, striking near the road to Vitry. I circled twice over the wreckage but could see no movement.

I was then forced to retire as the other two planes had maneuvered into position above me and were about to attack. Subsequently I learned that the pilot of the plane I had engaged was named Taylor and that he was a Lieutenant of the Royal Flying Corps. He had been instantly killed by a bullet through the heart. His machine was a de Havilland A9409 equipped with one Maxim gun."[49]

Udet had killed 2Lt. Robert Edward Taylor from No.41 Squadron, RFC, who crashed south of Izel-lès-Équerchin. His squadron mate, Lt. G.C. Holman, came down in the same vicinity in DH.5 A9410 as the victim of *Jasta* 30's *Uffz.* Emil Liebert. Udet confirmed this information when answering an inquiry from Taylor's family in 1931. He provided the same information as above, including Holman's death at the hands of a group of Albatroses from *Jasta* 30, and then added:

"About 1½ hours later I drove personally in a car to Izel and walked from there to the location, firstly to inspect the new type of DH.5 in detail and secondly to establish the name of the occupant. The airplane lay 50 meters west of the above-mentioned road [from Izel to Vitry], completely wrecked. With the help of some infantrymen the body of Lieutenant Taylor was taken from the machine; we took the papers, etc. from the body and I handed same (the papers, etc.) to the commander of the flying officers of the 6th Army Corps. Lieutenant Taylor had been shot through the heart and received serious injuries to the head, which was caused by his fall...Of the two discs carried by Lieutenant Taylor I took one away as a souvenir and left the other on the body which I wrapped in the tri-colour of his airplane wing. I further possess the map used by Lt. Taylor on his last flight and a small silver pocket mirror. I shall be glad to return these articles to his relatives, for whom the possession of these must be of far greater value than to me."[50]

Udet bagged his 12th on 24 September east of Loos. Described as a "lattice-tail two-seater" in Udet's combat report, no suitable candidate has been discovered by historians to date.[51] The *AOK 6* report

for the day related: *"Lt. Udet schoss 12^{20} 1 Nieuport über Loos brennend ab. Fl. liegt jenseits."* ("*Lt.* Udet shot down 1 Nieuport in flames over Loos at 12:20 p.m. The airplane lies on the other side of the lines." The fact that it did not fall into German hands might account for the discrepancy in type identification (a Sopwith did not have a lattice tail). Moreover, it might never have been recorded as downed by the Allies if the crew had landed safely.

Udet ended his tour at Phalempin airfield with a double victory on 28 September. He had taken off to intercept an artillery spotter when he came across a flight of five Sopwith Camels:

"The five flew in a wedge shape, that is the lead airplane lay in front with the rest following behind him staggered to the left and right. Since I came from above, I had greater speed and flew into the open end of the wedge. When I was so close that the two farthest airplanes flew in a line with me, only 30 to 40 meters to the right and left, I shot at the airplane closest to the left of the leader, which immediately went up in flames and went down. The next moment, I had the leader dead in my sights and riddled his engine and fuel tank with a few shots,

Facing Page: A rarely seen portrait of Udet.

apparently wounding him too because he stood his machine on its head and went down almost vertically. His landing ensued a few hundred meters behind our first line. The airplane was destroyed by our artillery. The other three Tommies were so shocked that they spun down in all directions. Unfortunately, I couldn't catch any more because I was following the leader; I thought his [descent] was a ruse and I did not want to let him get home over the front. This had been my first double."[52]

The Camels were from No.43 Squadron, RFC. The first was B6209, flown by 2Lt. R.P. Hood who crashed to his death west of Wingles. Capt. T.S. Wynn was in B2366 which was forced down near Vermelles with a shot-up engine. Wynn was uninjured, however, and managed to make it back to his lines to fight another day.

New Responsibilities

Jasta 37 moved north to Wynghene (today's Wingene), Belgium on 7 October and Udet was able to add to his scoresheet just 11 days later when he claimed a Sopwith Camel at 10:35 a.m. (9:35 British time) near Deûlémont. The only Camel brought down on 18 October 1917 did not even take off until 11:45 a.m., but as historian Trevor Henshaw has pointed out in *The Sky Their Battlefield II*, SE.5a B528 departed from No.56 Squadron's base at 8:10 a.m. and was subsequently engaged in battle with an enemy aircraft just north of Bas-Warneton – only a little over two kilometers northeast of Deûlémont – before it went missing. Its pilot, Lt. J.D. Gilbert, was killed in action and perhaps he was Udet's 14th victim.[53] Udet may have described the fight in the chapter titled *"Der erstaunte Sopwith-Flieger"* ("The Astonished Sopwith Flier"), given that it it immediately followed his "first double" narrative:

"I was back at *'Olympia Riesenhöhe'* ['tremendous Olympic heights'] across the lines in the neighborhood of Y. when I noticed far below one of our artillery airplanes on our side being followed and pressed down by two Englishmen. I immediately shut off the fuel, quickly put the machine on its nose, and hurtled down. When I was at about 2,000 meters' altitude, both Tommies were only at about 1,600 meters altitude and about two kilometers behind our good old LVG on our side of the lines. One of them seemed to see me because he immediately broke off, pushed hard to the west, and flew over our front at a very low height, whereas the other one first noticed me only when it was

Above: A candid snapshot of Udet relaxing in a courtyard.

too late. Then I realized from his flying that I was obviously dealing with a rank beginner. He flew straight toward the west. Since he was significantly slower than me, I quickly caught up to him and flew up close. I saw the pilot turn, terrified and staring at my airplane as if he had been hypnotized. He didn't think about turning or other antics and seemed to be waiting for my fusillade. Maybe he was armored and believed himself invincible. This is known to have happened before. I shot from scarcely 40 meters and shortly afterwards the Englishman's left wing broke away; it would have hurtled into my wings if I hadn't quickly banked to the right. The opponent came down about 500 meters on our side of the lines, killed by a shot to the chest."[54]

"Y." may have stood for Ypres and Deûlémont indeed was about half a kilometer behind the German lines. We also know that this fight occurred in the morning, because Udet subsequently related:

Above: Udet after he had returned to base following his parachute ordeal on 29 June 1918. Note the gas mask that someone from the 16th Infantry Regiment had given him. *Lt.* Heinrich Drekmann is at right.

"To balance out my morning success, I myself was shot down that afternoon."[55] Udet explained that he was visited by *Offz-Stv.* Julius Buckler, who "had done astonishingly well recently."[56] After having lunch together, Buckler headed home for his base at Wasquehal and Udet accompanied him partway before turning north along the front. Flak fire caught his attention and he spotted an RE.8 conducting artillery spotting below him at 1,500 meters' altitude. The RE.8 saw him and turned back toward the west. Udet was 300 meters or so above him and was about to attack when he suddenly felt a blow to his left leg and a stream of fuel erupted from his tank. He had been hit in the engine and fuel tank, and a ricochet had struck the gaiter on his leg without piercing it. Within seconds, his propeller stopped and Udet realized that at some four kilometers behind enemy lines, he had just enough altitude to make it over the German lines. He began his glide home only to discover to his dismay that

"a whole horde of Sopwith single-seaters" were passing over him. Three of them spotted him and went on the attack. He thought sure that he was doomed because he could do little more than "fly like a lame duck" a little to the right and a little to the left to evade them. Any stronger evasive maneuver would have cost him the altitude he need to get home. Fortunately for him, it appears that his pursuers were "rank beginners" because they fired at him only from 300 meters away and 200 meters above him. He managed to make it over his lines without further harm but then had to touch down in a flooded ditch. He crawled out of his cockpit along the top of the fuselage to avoid getting soaked and was rescued by the leader of a nearby flak battery who took him into his dugout just before British artillery opened up on his downed fighter. After a difficult journey home via foot, horse, and auto, Udet returned to his airfield the next morning. Udet closed his account with:

"The flight activity gradually lessened and times grew more peaceful in the winter. I became the leader of a *Jagdstaffel* and decided to fly together with my gentlemen from now on..."[57]

Jasta 37's CO, *Oblt.* Kurt Grasshoff, departed on 7 November to take command of *Jasta* 38 in Macedonia. Before leaving, however, he made sure that Udet was the man who would replace him. Grasshoff also probably recommended Udet for the Royal Hohenzollern House Order, Knight's Cross with Swords, that was bestowed upon him on 13 November.

Udet scored successes on 28 November, 5 December 1917, and 6 January 1918, all of which have been tentatively identified. The two that followed on 28 and 29 January 1918, however, have been a mystery to historians. His claim report (see the images on pages 24–25) from 28 January read:

"My *Kette* [small flight] was attacked at about 4,600 meters by several S.E.5s in the vicinity of Klerken. An S.E.5 with pennants on its tail plunged down behind *Vzfw.* Schulz but I immediately attacked and shot at him. First, I drove him down to about 900 meters on this side of the lines. Then the Englishman straightened out a bit and flew hard towards Houthulst Forest with me shooting him. After he had flown for a short distance, he suddenly fell quite steeply to the ground, without righting himself, in the crater field west of Houthulst Forest."

Notes on the second page related: "Ground

Above: This grainy image shows Udet inspecting the wreckage of 1Lt. Walter Wanamaker's Nieuport 28, downed on 2 July 1918. (photo courtesy of Greg VanWyngarden)

observation not obtained because of strong haze," and that no further information on the downed aircraft was ascertainable because it had gone down on the other side of the lines. Thus it may very well have gotten away.

Udet's all-important 20th confirmed victory – the one that would technically qualify him for the *Pour le Mérite* – fell on 18 February 1918 near Zandvoorde. He recalled it in a chapter titled "*Der zwanzigste Luftsieg*" ("The 20th Air Victory"):

"On a beautiful, sunny December [*sic*] morning, I flew along the front at a very high altitude with five aircraft from my *Staffel*. Enemy activity was quite low, and apart from a *Kette* [small group] of five single-seat fighters flying below us far away on the other side, there was nothing to see. To attract the enemy, I flew a bit on the other side, turned around about 400 meters above the Tommies, and slowly headed southwest toward our front, always keeping an eye out for any Englishmen coming after us. In this way, I wanted to pull them across our territory

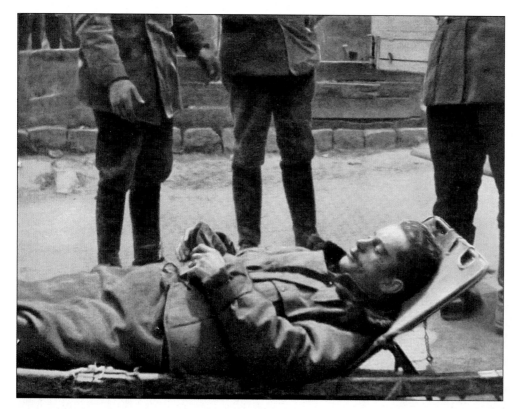

somewhat to gain the advantage in a fight. We were headed straight into the sun, and I covered it with my thumb as I always do when looking into its light. Then – I could hardly believe my eyes – about 100 meters in front of us, heading straight for us, were eight Sopwith single-seaters who apparently had not seen us earlier. They were about 50 meters higher than we were, but the lowest was exactly at my altitude. It took just a second to get him in my sights and shoot. He immediately hurtled down like a plumb line…One really can't have it any easier than when an enemy flies into one's mouth like a roasted bird – or in this case, like an unroasted one in front of one's machine gun."[58]

The unfortunate Camel pilot, FSLt. R.E. Burr in RNAS No.10 Squadron's N6347, was wounded in action, came down just inside the British lines, and died of his wounds two days later. This would prove to be Udet's final victory with *Jasta 37*.

Richthofen

Udet began his *Kreuz wider Kokarde* chapter on Richthofen with:

"I was invited to lunch by Richthofen. I had met him before and was looking forward to the afternoon. I arrived at his *Geschwader* after a long car ride. I saw a sign hanging on a tiny little dilapidated wooden shack: '*Rittmeister Freiherr* von Richthofen,

Jagdgeschwader Commander." This was how our most outstanding aviator lived."[59]

In a story published in *Vossische Zeitung* on 21 April 1933 – the 15th anniversary of Richthofen's death – Udet explained how they had first met:

"It has been four months since I visited his *Geschwader* on the town of Courtrai in Flanders. An unpleasant matter led me to visit him. In his enthusiasm, a pilot from my *Staffel* had mixed up friend and foe and attacked a triplane of the *Staffel* led by Richthofen. Richthofen had spared me from having to make any sort of explanation during this somewhat embarrassing visit to seek atonement. While he showed some understanding for the excessive zeal of my young comrade, his anger focused on the command post responsible, which had neglected to inform the army's flying units that after a long pause triplanes were again being flown on the German side and not only on the enemy's side."[60]

In his later *Mein Fliegerleben*, Udet explained how they had become reacquainted. Udet was helping his mechanics erect aircraft tents in the pouring rain at their new airfield outside of Le Cateau (*Jasta 37* relocated there on 15 March 1918) when he felt a tap on his back. When he turned around, he was face to face with a dripping wet Manfred von Richthofen, who greeted Udet and inquired about the number of aircraft he had downed. Udet replied that he had 19 confirmed, one pending, to which Richthofen responded:

"Hm, twenty then. Then you would actually seem ripe for us. Would you like to?"[61]

Udet replied to this nonchalant invitation to join *JG* I with an enthusiastic "Yes!" A week or so later, he was having lunch with Richthofen:

"I was most heartily welcomed by him at the Officers' Mess, and we thoroughly enjoyed a deliciously prepared meal. I knew most of the gentlemen in his *Staffel* from before. After lunch, Richthofen told me that he still needed a *Staffelführer* for his *Geschwader* and offered the post to me. I was of course all fired up to work under him and three days later was a *Staffelführer* in the Richthofen *Geschwader*."[62]

Richthofen's brother, Lothar, had been leading *Jasta* 11 when he was seriously injured in a crash on 13 March. During his absence, Udet was made the unit's acting CO on 24 March. He showed Richthofen and the men of *JG* I what he was made of just three days later. On 27 March, Richthofen was leading a *Geschwader* flight when:

"An RE, a British artillery spotter, hangs just below the clouds above the ruins of Albert. Probably ranging his batteries. We are a bit lower than he, but he apparently hasn't noticed us, because he quietly continues to circle. I exchange a quick glance with Scholtz; he nods. I separate from the *Staffel* and race for the 'Tommy.' I take him on from the front. I dart at him like a shark from below and fire at short range. His engine is riddled like a sieve. He immediately tilts over and right after that bursts apart in the air. The burning debris crashes down close to Albert."[63]

Udet's victim may have been No.42 Squadron RE.8 B6528, which left its base at 10:50 a.m. (Udet's claim was at 11:50 a.m.) and was initially reported as missing in action. It turned out that its occupants, Lt. J.V.R. Brown and 2Lt. C.F. Warren, had both been wounded in action and had crashed, but were later discovered to be in British hands after the MIA report had been filed. If they were felled by Udet, then his postwar recollection that their aircraft had disintegrated in midair was incorrect.[64]

Udet found success again the next day:

Above: 1Lt. Walter Wanamaker. (photo courtesy of Greg VanWyngarden)

"On March 28 I am under way with Gussmann… Suddenly, an Englishman is above us. He plunges at Gussmann, Gussmann dodges, pushes down…I lift my head for a moment and see a second Englishman rushing at me. He is barely 150 meters away. He opens fire at 80 meters. It is impossible to avoid him, so I fly straight toward him. Tack-tack-tack barks my machine gun, tack-tack-tack barks his back. Just 20 meters distance. It looks like our machines will ram each other in another second. Then, a small movement, and he barely jumps over me. His propwash shakes me, the smell of castor oil wafts over me. I make a tight turn. 'Now the dogfight begins,' I think. But he has also turned, and we, firing, charge right at each other again like two tournament knights with couched lances. This time I fly over him. Another turn. Again, he is straight across from me, and once more we pounce on each other. The thin, white trails of tracer ammunition hang in the air like curtains. He sweeps over me with barely a hand's width to spare…'8224' it says in

652
Postkartenvertrieb W.Sanke
BERLIN N.37.
Nachdruck wird gerichtlich verfolgt.

Unser erfolgreicher Kampfflieger
Leutnant Udet

Left & Facing Page: While attending the July 1918 fighter evaluations that followed the Second Fighter Competition at Adlershof, Udet had these formal portraits taken at either E. Bieber's or Nicola Perscheid's studio in Berlin (various copies of these images have been attributed to both). As seen here, they were later featured on Sanke postcards.

653
Postkartenvertrieb W.Sanke
BERLIN N.37.
Nachdruck wird gerichtlich verfolgt.

Unser erfolgreicher Kampfflieger
Leutnant Udet

Facing Page: This is the original photograph before it was artistically edited to produce the first image on page 40.

Above: The first of three portraits of Udet in the field.

black numerals on his airplane's fuselage. A fourth time. I can feel my hands getting damp. That fellow over there is a man who is fighting the fight of his life. Him or me...one of us will remain standing... there is no other way out. For the fifth time! The nerves are stretched to the breaking point, but the head works coldly and clearly. This time the matter has to be settled. I line him up in my sights, head for him, right at him. I am resolved not to give an inch...We race at each other like wild boars. If he keeps his nerve this time, we will both be lost! Then, he turns off, avoids me. At that moment, my volley hits him. His apparatus rears up, turns on its back, and disappears in a gigantic crater. A fountain of earth, smoke...Twice I circle the place where he fell. Field grays are standing below, waving at me, shouting.

I have never concerned myself with the opponents I have shot down. He who fights must not look at the wounds he makes. But this time I want to know who the other guy was. Toward evening, at dusk, I drive off. A field hospital is close to where he crashed. They probably took him there. I ask for the doctor. He comes. His white gown shines ghostly in the glaring light of the carbide lamp. The other guy had been shot in the head, died instantaneously. The doctor hands me his wallet. Calling cards: 'Lieutenant C.R. Maasdorp, Ontario RFC 47.' So, from the Royal Flying Corps. A picture of an old woman and a letter. 'You musn't fly so many sorties. Think of your father and me.' A medic brings me the number of the aircraft. He had cut it out. It is covered with small flecks of blood. I drive back to the *Staffel.* One must not think about the fact that a mother will cry for each man one shoots down."[65]

2Lt. Charles Roland Maasdorp was shot down in Sopwith Camel C8224 and crashed somewhere between Thiepval and Courcelette. He was serving with No.43 Squadron, and not No.47, at the time. Udet kept the serial number from Maasdorp's Camel and hung it up on the wall of his apartment in Berlin after the war.

Udet began to suffer from ear pains and was sent to *Kriegslazarett* (War Hospital) 7 in Valenciennes for treatment.[66] He was back in the air on 6 April and managed to bring down Lt. H.S. Lewis in No.43 Squadron's Sopwith Camel C8247 near Hamel that day. *Jasta* mate *Lt.* Richard Wenzl provided this anecdote about Udet's 23rd:

"I made my next takeoff under Udet, who was in charge of *Jasta* 11 and had 22 kills. He was going on leave to see his girlfriend and was eager to shoot down one more so that the *"Blaue Max"* (= *Pour le Mérite*) would be a sure thing. Accordingly, he dragged us along on this flight and flew his fuel tank dry until he finally shot down a Sopwith Camel in flames."[67]

Home Leave and *Pour le Mérite*

Udet visited the family doctor upon his arrival and was informed that his flying days were over due to a burst eardrum and inner ear infection. Depressed by the doctor's prognosis, he was soon buoyed by momentous news:

"One evening, however, all the windows are still lit. I go up the stairs, the hallway door is open, and my mother appears in the doorway. Her face is red and shining with joy, and she is waving a piece of paper in her hand. A telegram has arrived, a telegram from the *Geschwader.* They opened it. I've gotten the *Pour le Mérite.* I'm happy, really happy, although it isn't a complete surprise...But a really deep, inner heartfelt joy ignites my mother's happiness. She is completely beside herself and has forced everyone to

Above: The second of three portraits of Udet in the field. (photo courtesy of Greg VanWyngarden)

Right: The third of three portraits of Udet in the field. He is wearing a leather flight coat that was "liberated" from a British airman.

stay up and wait for me. Even my little sister."[68]

The official date of the award was 9 April 1918. In celebration, his mother cut a medal out of paper and hung it from his throat with a piece of yarn, while his father opened "a bottle of Steinberger Kabinett, 1884 vintage, one of the family heirlooms."[69]

The next morning, he thought how he would surprise his sweetheart, Eleonore "Lo" Zink. But when he tried to pick up a *Pour le Mérite* from Gebrüder Hemmerle, Munich's premier jeweler,

he was told that there was none to be had.[70] After leaving the store, however, he by chance ran into *Kptlt.* Ralph Wenninger, CO of U-Boat *UB 55*, who was on leave in his native Munich after having been granted his own *Pour le Mérite* on 30 March. Udet spotted the decoration dangling from Wenninger's throat and asked if he happened to have a second one he could spare. The submariner was somewhat taken aback but then laughed long and hard after Udet explained that he wanted to impress his girlfriend. Wenninger did not have a spare but said he could

give Udet the address of a Berlin jeweler from whom a *Pour le Mérite* could be ordered by telegram. Udet did so and the decoration arrived a few days later.[71]

Lo was thrilled when he, wearing Prussia's highest award for bravery, collected her at her home for a morning date. The couple went for a stroll around the center of Munich and as they passed in front of the *Residenz* (the King of Bavaria's palace), one of its sentries suddenly cried out:

"'Guard. Fall out!' The men dash out like the devil. 'Fall in,' commands the officer. 'Attention!..Shoulder arms! Ready! Present Arms!' I look around. Nobody is near. Then I remember my *Pour le Mérite*. I am almost past when I return the salute. It comes off quite poorly, too hasty and without dignity. 'What was that all about?' asks Lo, looking at me with big eyes. 'God,' I say as casually as possible, 'the Guard has to fall out before a *Pour le Mérite*.' 'You're kidding!' 'No, I'm not!' 'Good, then let's try it again.'"[72]

Meanwhile, back at *JG* I, Udet was officially replaced by *Lt.* Hans Weiss as the Acting CO of *Jasta* 11 on 18 April, the same day that Udet's transfer to *JG* I was officially approved and backdated to 5 April.[73] This may seem strange at first, considering that Udet had been with the *Geschwader* since 24 March, but it

was probably only a case of the bureaucracy catching up with actual events.

Udet found time to attend the *Deutsche Luftkriegsbeute Ausstellung* (German Airwar Booty Exhibition, or *DELKA*) which had been put on in Berlin and Dresden before moving to Munich in April 1918.[74] There he met with *DELKA*'s director, Ernst Friedrich Eichler, who pitched the idea of an autobiography to Udet and later assembled and published *Kreuz wider Kokarde*. A photograph of the two of them at the exhibition was featured in that work (opposite p.32).

On 22 April, Udet and Lo were walking near the National Theater when they noticed a crowd gathering around a news poster. Believing at first that it was probably another victory announcement, Udet was shocked to read the headline: "*Rittmeister Freiherr* von Richthofen Missing!":

"The letters waver uncertainly in front of my eyes. I see no one and pay attention to no one as I ruthlessly elbow my way through the crowd to the front row. Fifty centimeters in front of me, the yellowish-white piece of paper is pasted to the wall: 'Did not return from a sortie against the enemy. Investigations inconclusive so far.' And then I know, know with

Above & Below: These images originated during a visit by Udet to the Pfalz factory in Speyer. In the first (left to right): *Oblt*. Seibert, *Lt*. Hans Klein, Alfred Everbusch (Pfalz Company Owner), Udet, *Lt*. Constantin Krefft, *Oblt*. Lucas (Austrian Air Service), Dr. Otto Moericke (Mayor of Speyer). Pfalz D.XII 2603/18 is behind them. In the second, Seibert is third from left, Udet is fifth from left follwed by Alfred Everbusch and Hans Klein. (first photo courtesy of Jack Herris)

Above: This snapshot originated around 6 October 1918, when Udet, flying Siemens-Schuckert (SSW) D.III 8350/17, held a mock dogfight with Friedrich Noltenius at Metz-Frescaty airdrome (see page 137). According to its caption, left to right: Müller, unknown, Udet, von Barnekow (a relative of Raven von Barnekow?), (Julius) Schulte-Frohlinde, (Erich) von Wedel, (Hermann) Göring, SSW engineer Kaendler.

Left & Facing Page: Udet attended the Third Fighter Competition held at Adlershof from 10 to 28 October 1918. These photos were among several that captured him there. In the first, he is in flight gear standing next to *Hptm.* Bruno Loerzer. The second is a group photo of *Pour le Mérite* pilots (Boenigk received his within days of this photo) with Alfred Everbusch, one of the founders of the Pfalz Aircraft Company. Standing (left to right): *Lt.* Hans Klein, *Lt.* Josef Veltjens, Everbusch, Udet, *Lt.* Josef Jacobs. Seated (left to right): *Oblt.* Hermann Göring, *Hptm.* Bruno Loerzer, *Oblt.* Oskar von Boenigk.

unerring certainty, that the *Rittmeister* is dead."[75]

Udet was right. Richthofen had been shot down and killed the day before and had already been buried in Bertangles, France when the news spread to Germany. Udet, no doubt suffering from "survivor's guilt," grew increasingly restless and pressed the doctor for an update on his condition. The doctor responded that the ear infection had abated but that complete recuperation was still very much needed. But that was all Udet needed to hear and he reported back to *JG* I sometime after the middle of May.[76]

Back in the Fight

Udet was transferred from *Jasta* 11 to *Jasta* 4 on 21 May and took over as that unit's CO the next day. On the night of the 26th, *JG* I was moved to Ferme de Puisieux (5 kilometers northeast of Laon along the road from Chambry to Monceau-le-Waast) to support Operation Blücher, or the Third Battle of the

Aisne, when it commenced the next day.

Udet brought down his 24th victory – a Breguet XIV from *Escadrille Br* 29 southwest of Soissons – on 31 May. He and *Lt.* Viktor von Pressentin *gen* von Rautter claimed two Breguets within minutes of each other southwest of Soissons, and the death certificates for two *Escadrille Br* 29 crews downed in combat that day appear to offer their identities. They state that *Sgt.* Hippolyte Julien Martin and *Sol.* Jean René Galbrun were killed near Dommiers while their squadron mates, *Sous-Lt.* Charles Maurice Béranger and *Sgt.* Edouard Simon Wolf, came down near Missy-aux-Bois.[77] Dommiers and Missy-aux-Bois are adjacent to one another just 4 kilometers southwest of Soissons.

JG I occupied the former French airfield east of Beugneux on 1 June. Udet racked up another 16 victories from this location before going back to Germany for several weeks in July. He described only four of those 16 successes in his books, but

Left: Udet in full regalia. His *Grossordensschnalle* (medals bar) displays (left to right): Iron Cross, 2nd Class; Royal Hohenzollern House Order, Knight's Cross with Swords; Merit Cross with Swords (Württemberg); Hanseatic Cross (Hamburg); Hanseatic Cross (Lübeck). The decorations pinned to his tunic below them are (left to right): Iron Cross, 1st Class; Pilot's Badge; Wound Badge in Silver.

we can now supplement those passages with information regarding the remainder, including some who have hitherto gone unidentified.

On 2 June, *Sgt*. Marcel Charles Ernest Commandeur and *Sgt*. Marcel Hedman were sent in an *Escadrille Br* 108 Breguet XIV to bomb Villers-Petit (just north of Chouy) and Neuilly-Saint-Front. They were shot down during the raid and, according

Right: Udet and Eleonore "Lo" Zink.

to their death certificates, crashed in the vicinity of Passy-en-Valois, just 3 kilometers west of Neuilly-Saint-Front where Udet claimed a Breguet as his 25th.

Udet was awarded a SPAD south of Buzancy on 5 June for his 26th. Two SPAD VIIs from *Escadrille Spa* 62 were shot down near Vierzy, only 3 kilometers to the southwest: *Sgt.* André Bernard in 7216 (taken prisoner) and *Sous-Lt.* Charles Quette in 5603 (killed in action). Either one could have been Udet's victim.[78]

Udet put in for another SPAD fighter south of Faverolles on 6 June. A recent examination of death certificates tells us that *Sgt.* Jean Pierre Louis Alfred Bouilliant from *Escadrille Spa* 69 was "killed by the enemy" that day "at Faverolles (Aisne)." He may well have been Udet's 27th.

On the evening of 7 June, a third SPAD fell before his guns east of Villers-Cotterêts at 7:00 p.m. (6:00 French time). *Escadrille Spa* 86 lost a SPAD VII at 6:00 p.m. that was being flown by a Japanese citizen and volunteer in the French Air Service, *Sgt.* Kobayashi Shukunosuke. It was noted that he had gone down in the vicinity of Montgobert, some six kilometers northeast of Villers-Cotterêts; so he is a possible candidate for Udet's 28th success.

Udet continued his run on SPADs by shooting another down northwest of Faverolles on 13 June.

There was a lot of action that day with *Spas* 75, 77, and 98 reporting five SPADs with wounded, missing, or killed pilots in that vicinity. Any one could have been Udet's victim; however, he and *Jasta* mate *Lt.* Heinrich Drekmann brought two SPADs down at the same time (5:45 p.m. German time) with Drekmann's falling northeast of Noroy-sur-Ourcq. We might therefore presume that they were from the same French unit. If so, then their victims may have been *Cpl.* Jacques Edmond Chapal (reportedly killed near Troësnes) and *Brig.* François Aleppe of *Spa* 98.

Udet's 30th the next day, over yet another SPAD, might have been *Spa* 163's *Sous-Lt.* Marie Majon de la Débuterie, who was taken prisoner and was the only SPAD reported as shot down that day; however, we currently have too little information about his downing to firmly connect them.

Two Breguets were claimed by Udet on 23 June. One of them, near Crouy, was almost certainly *Escadrille Br* 216's *Lt.* Pierre François Hilaire Félicien Tournadre and *Sol.* Pic in a Breguet XIV. Tournadre's death certificate relates that he was killed at "Fussy near Crouy-sur-Ourcq." The only other Breguet shot down that day belonged to *Br* 237 with *Sous-Lt.* Marchand and *Sol.* Forest as its crew. Again, however, we have too little else to go on to securely link them to Udet.

Udet's 33rd fell on 24 June and he had this to say about it:

"We went down on them in a powered-off glide and quickly recognized them as Breguet two-seaters who seemed to be coming home from directing their artillery, thinking about anything other than their being attacked by *Boches* in the next few seconds over their tethered balloons. Two, however, realized what was going on at just the last moment and took their leave by diving down; yet the third seemed braver and met my attack. He turned to approach me, but I had quickly caught up to him and now hung directly behind and below his tail. After a well-aimed volley, the airplane curved down to the right and flew directly under me. I immediately followed and saw that the pilot, with head tipped back, sat in his seat while the observer lay stretched out on the bottom of his cockpit; so both were dead and the crate still flew – sometimes to the left, sometimes to the right – as the wind drove it, slowly losing altitude. I tried everything to set it on fire but only had success after 200 shots from close range. The Breguet with its dead crew began to burn lightly from under its fuselage but still flew normally to the south. Gradually, however, the fire grew rampant and in a great, widely-visible blaze the airplane broke apart at about 400 meters' altitude; the charred remains fell near an enemy tethered balloon, which by that time had been pulled down to the ground."[79]

Udet reported that his victim came down "southeast of Montigny." Some sources have offered that an *Escadrille Br* 128 Breguet manned by *Sgt.* Samuel Jean Cachard and *Sgt.* Jules Emile Morel was Udet's 33rd victim. Their death certificates state that they were killed in air combat "east of Vierzy." Vierzy is 20 km northeast of Montigny-l'Allier and 12 km southeast of Montigny-Lengrain, both of which seem somewhat far away from where the *Br* 128 crew were reportedly killed. Moreover, Cachard and Morel were initially listed as missing in action, which implies that they were brought down in German territory (such as east of Vierzy) rather than over French territory near one of their balloons. A better candidate can be found with the aircraft flown by *Cpt.* François Pierre Paul Fageol and *Lt.* Marie Daniel Eugène Faure. The death certificates for both men relate that they were killed in action around 9:15 a.m. "near Cœuvres." Udet's claim was recorded as around 10:00 a.m. (9:00 French time) southeast of Montigny. Cœuvres-et-Valsery is immediately southeast of Montigny-Lengrain and both were just behind the French lines according to maps of the Western Front in June 1918. The problem has been that the men have been listed as flying a 20th *Corps d'Armée* Salmson 2A2 – not a Breguet XIV. French air historian Christophe Cony has discovered through further research that the 20th *Corps d'Armée* consisted of *Sal* 70, *Sal* 253, and *Br* 35. Fageol and Faure belonged to *Br* 35 so they were in fact flying a Breguet XIV when they were shot down near Cœuvres-et-Valsery. This would appear to make the match complete.

In a chapter erroneously titled "*Meine zweite Dublette*" ("My Second Double"), Udet described what was actually his third double victory, 25 June 1918. Leading a *Jasta* 4 patrol during his second front flight of the evening, Udet became disappointed when he found that none of the enemy machines they had approached wanted to engage in battle:

"I was just about to fly home with my *Staffel* when I noticed a SPAD formation coming from the north and approaching the lines. It was about 500 meters lower than us and we immediately went over to attack. Over the great forest of X., I began a closer acquaintance with the lead airplane which slowly, but surely, curved down to the forest. The opponent defended himself with all his might, but it was no use. At about 400 meters' altitude, I shot up his motor so that his propeller stopped; another well-aimed volley finished him off, and the SPAD went

Above: Udet and Eleonore "Lo" Zink.

down vertically into the forest. When he disappeared in the trees and I wanted to enjoy my victory, I noticed a second SPAD approaching me in a dive from above. The situation was critical for me in that I was about one kilometer over the lines and only 50-100 meters above the forest. At first, I flew straight ahead for a short distance and pretended that I hadn't noticed the man who so vigorously was out for my blood; at the same time, I pushed my machine to get up as much speed as possible. At the exact moment that he got into good firing distance from me, I pulled my machine into a right-angled, righthand turn, however, and flew straight at him from the front. He didn't seem to be prepared for that. His movements became uncertain, and instead of shooting ahead at me, he tried turning in front of me to fly back toward the west. That put me in a good firing position, and after a volley of 20 shots, a large tongue of flame shot out from the SPAD's fuselage, but it went out again right afterwards. Suddenly, he was in a hurry to land and went straight down in a shallow glide to a forest clearing that had just come into our possession. Despite shell holes and other obstacles, he made a very neat landing under my supervision."[80]

Both of Udet's victims were from *Escadrille Spa 96*. The first was American William Vernon Booth, Jr., whose final fight was described in a 1922 publication:

"On June 25, above the fighting to the south of Soissons, Booth was engaged in bitter combat with a swarm of Fokkers. Hemmed in, outnumbered and maneuvering desperately, always on the offensive, Booth's machine was suddenly set on fire by an incendiary bullet, and at the same instant an explosive ball shattered his right leg, inflicting a terrible wound. Enveloped in flames and in an agony of pain, he still kept his head, and after a straight plunge of 6000 feet succeeded in putting out the fire. But by now the motor had stopped for good, forcing him to land near Longpont, by misfortune at a point exactly between the lines, forty yards from the Germans – thirty from the French. The Germans promptly turned rifles, machine guns, and even 37 mm. cannon on the Spad, but in spite of a storm of lead and bursting shell, severely burned and dragging a mangled leg, Booth painfully extricated himself from his plane, deliberately set fire to what was left of it, and crawled to the French lines. In the hospital, on July 4, this splendid act of courage was rewarded with the *Médaille Militaire*, and on July 10 Booth died from the effects of his wounds."[81]

Booth's wife was at his side when he expired at the Scottish Women's Hospital at Asnières-sur-Oise. The second unfortunate airman was *Cpl.* Edouard Aury, who was also wounded in action. He too landed, made it back to his own lines, but survived his wounds.

Udet had a harrowing experience that he wrote about in both *Kreuz wider Kokarde* and *Mein Fliegerleben*.[82] But Karl Bodenschatz, *JG* I's Adjutant, published Udet's original report:

"On 29 June 1918, I took off at 7:15 a.m. with my *Staffel* on a hunting flight. At 7:40 a.m. over Cutry, I attacked an infantry-support plane flying at an altitude of 800 meters over the area which was under heavy French shell fire. Upon my first attack, the Breguet turned towards me and flew under me. As he did so, I observed that the observer was no longer standing in his machine-gun ring. I therefore assumed I had already hit the observer and, contrary to my usual habit, I attacked the enemy pilot from the flank. I suddenly noticed, however, that the French observer had reappeared from the body of the plane and, at that same moment, I took several hits, including one in the machine gun and another in the fuel tank. At the same time, the elevator and aileron cable must have been shot through, because my Fokker D VII plunged out of control. I tried everything possible – sometimes with the throttle, sometimes with the rudder – to bring the plane under control, but in vain. At an altitude of about 500 meters, the machine went over on its nose and I could no longer bring it out of this position. It was high time to get out. I unbuckled myself, positioned myself up on the seat, and in the next moment, I was flung backwards by a tremendous draught of air. At the same time, I felt a violent jerk and realized that I had gotten hung up by my parachute on the leading edge of the rudder. Summoning up the last of my strength, I broke the tip off and I fell free behind the airplane, repeatedly tumbling head over heels. I had already assumed that the parachute had malfunctioned when I suddenly felt a slight braking and shortly after that hit the ground. The chute had opened after all at about 80 meters. The landing was pretty hard and I sprained my left leg. I had come down west of Cutry in the middle of a heavy barrage. The enemy fired on me with machine guns shortly before and after landing. I unbuckled myself from the parachute and ran in an easterly direction. Just then I received a hard blow to the back of the head and was knocked to the ground by a blast of air. Apparently, a dirt clod thrown up by the impact of a large-caliber shell had hit me. Shortly after that, my left cheek

Above: Udet (third from left) and *Hptm*. Bruno Loerzer (third from right) pose with an American military delegation soon after the war. Friedrich Seekatz from the Fokker Company is second from the left. This image originated the same time as the one seen on page 54 of Volume 14 of this series.

was hit by a small stone also thrown up by the numerous shells impacting around me. I ran with all my might and luckily came to the edge of the ravine north of Missy[-aux-Bois], where I was taken in by the 16th Infantry Regiment. I experienced heavy coughing and nausea, as I had covered the distance of roughly three kilometers without a gas mask. After about three hours, the gas attack let up; I was able to reach the Paris road and from there, Courmelles, where I was able to communicate with the *Geschwader* by telephone. I was picked up in a car and by that afternoon I was able to carry out a more auspicious hunting flight."[83]

Udet quickly recovered from the incident and bagged his 36th victory – a SPAD near Faverolles – the very next day. His victim may have been *Escadrille Spa* 73's *Lt*. Bernard Charles Marie Alfred de Girval, whose death certificate states that he was killed in a plane crash in the vicinity of Bonneuil-en-Valois, some 13 km. west of Faverolles. Other sources say that he was killed in combat over the Forêt de Retz, which separates the two sites. On the other hand,

Udet might have shot down *Escadrille Spa* 87's *Sous-Lt.* Jean Onézime Lavergne, who went missing in the vicinity of Muizon.

Motor magazine (May-June 1919) published an article by Udet that was translated as "My Experiences with the B.M.W. Motor Type IIIa" by Alex Imrie.[84] In it, Udet related:

"On the 1st of July, 1918 at about 11 a.m., the two of us [Udet and *Lt*. Heinrich Drekmann] flew over Longpont (southwest of Soissons) at 19,000 feet. About 1,000 feet above us a French Breguet two-seater was just about to cross our lines. Obviously, he had been watching us because he turned westwards and flew back behind his lines, and I followed, gradually overhauling him. Instead of diving the Breguet climbed, and in a few minutes we were both at 21,000 feet, and I was about 100 yards behind him. Northwest of the forest of Villers-Cotterêts I opened fire, and in a few seconds the Breguet went down in flames."

Above: Udet (left) and Robert *Ritter* von Greim flew together in airshows throughout Germany during August--October 1919. This candid photo originated during one of them. (photo courtesy of Reinhard Kastner)

Udet's claim was at 11:45 a.m. (10:45 French time) and the death certificate for *Br* 219's *Sous-Lt.* Pierre André Joseph Schalbar states that he was killed "at 11 h...near Villers-Cotterêts...in air combat." So there is little doubt that he and his pilot, *Lt.* Henri Dupont, were the crew of Udet's 37th success. His 38th fell later the same day – a SPAD east of Faverolles at 8:55 p.m. (7:55 French time). The only recorded SPAD candidate is *Spa* 98's *Sgt.* James Henry Baugham, an American who was said to have tangled with three Fokkers near Villers-Cotterêts and been wounded before limping back to friendly territory, where he died the next day. Villers-Cotterêts is indeed east of Faverolles; however, the

time of Baugham's action is given as 4:30 p.m., so unless one of the time records is wrong, we do not appear to have a match.

Udet told the tale of his fight and victory on 2 July in a chapter titled "*Der Amerikaner*" ("The American"). He was awakened by flak fire and took off to see what the commotion was all about. Then he saw a flight of Nieuports tangling with a *Kette* of Fokkers:

"When I soon came over the twisting and turning dogfight, I recognized Loewenhardt's machine which had just gotten a Nieuport 'under treatment.' A second opponent used that moment to push down behind Loewenhardt. During the course of this, he didn't count on my wriggling my way up to him in the meantime to join in, and before he knew it, he had received several shots from me close up through the motor and tank. He became quite flustered by this, immediately dove down, and tried in great haste to fly over the X. River that separated us from the French. I therefore had to go after him forcefully to dissuade him from that intention. He turned inland again and soon discovered in which direction he could continue his glide without my shooting at him. I only fired at him when he tried to get behind his lines again. As long as he made his way inland, I let him glide unmolested. While landing, my client seemed somewhat bewildered, sideslipped from a turn just above the ground, and had one hell of a crackup. I landed near him and went to his machine to find out more about the new Nieuport's design details. When I arrived at the wreckage, which carried the French tricolor, some infantrymen were pulling the pilot out. The man had broken his lower left leg in the crash and suffered several scratches and bruises, but was otherwise fine. We greeted each other with a handshake; when I spoke to him in French and he couldn't answer me in that language, I was delighted to discover that – despite the French cockades – I had been dealing with Americans and could now make the acquaintance of an American *Staffel* member. The representative of Uncle Sam behaved quite decently."[85]

The "new" Nieuport Udet referred to was the recently-introduced Nieuport 28 model. Udet had failed to discern that the cockade he had observed on it (red outer circle, blue inner circle, white center) was slightly different from the French version (red outer circle, white inner circle, blue center) because his opponent had been 1Lt. Walter B. Wanamaker of the 27th Aero Squadron, USAS. In any event, Udet cut the fabric bearing the Nieuport's serial number from its rudder as a souvenir and had Wanamaker sign it. After the war, Wanamaker gave his own brief account of his fight with Udet:

"There were eleven planes in the German squadron against our nine; but we went up after them. It was the most thrilling dog-fight I've ever seen and the second longest air fight of the war – 32 minutes. I suddenly discovered that a red Fokker was pouring lead into my plane, and I tried to evade him by going into a tail spin. But I couldn't fool him. A bullet struck my gas tank and another hit the propeller. Gas rushed into my face, my mouth and my lungs. Then I tried to go for the French lines, but the man I later learned to be Udet, was still hovering over me

and still firing. I couldn't make the French lines that way, so I turned and swooped down to the nearest open spot I could find. I don't know how I got out alive for the plane broke in two at the cockpit."[86]

Udet's claim of 3 July demonstrates the risks inherent in trying to determine who got whom. That day, two *Jasta* 6 pilots – *Vzfw.* Franz Hemer and *Lt.* Werner Nöldecke – claimed two SPADs. Hemer's fell east of Courtieux at 8:00 a.m. and Nöldecke's at 7:10 p.m. nearby. Two *Jasta* 4 pilots – Udet and *Lt.* Heinrich Drekmann – also claimed two SPADs, but theirs came down simultaneously at 8:25 a.m. east of Laversine (Udet) and northwest of Dommiers (Drekmann). [87] The pilots of two SPAD XIIIs from *Spa* 65 – *Adj.* Georges Eugène Antoine Lienhard and *Adj.* Jacques Gérard – were killed near Chaudun (Lienhard) and Missy[aux-Bois] (Gérard) but we do not know at what times. These locations are immediately east of Dommiers, which itself is just east of Laversine. Courtieux is eight kilometers west of Laversine and is even farther away from Dommiers/Chaudun/ Missy-aux-Bois; accordingly, we might have surmised that it was likely that Lienhard and Gérard were the victims of Udet and Drekmann. However, as it turns out, Gérard was credited to *Lt.* Werner Preuss of *Jasta* 66! Preuss had also claimed a SPAD that day, but no details were given as to when and where. Gérard was confirmed as his 3rd victory by the combined work of air historians Adam Wait, Greg VanWyngarden, and David Méchin. Wait translated an article by Preuss that had been published in a 1936 anthology titled *Propeller überm Feind.* In it, Preuss described how he saw a huge airfight over the lines that included a *Staffel* of the Richthofen *Geschwader.* Suddenly, a German machine dove away, pursued by two Frenchman who were firing furiously at him. As they grew closer, Preuss recognized Udet's "red machine" and decided to help him out, even though he might be accused of being an "*Aasjäger*" – literally, "a hunting bugger" or someone who steals a victory from a comrade. He dove at full speed after them, risking his life because of the strain he was placing on his aircraft, and managed to catch them. He got within an airplane length of one of the Frenchmen, fired for one or two seconds, but then had to pull up to avoid a collision. When he rejoined the fray, he saw that his victim had been badly shot up and was going down. He watched as he slammed into the ground and then observed Udet flying up to him from the same vicinity as his victim's crash site. When he drew alongside Preuss, it was clear that he was upset about something. Preuss thought: "Did I not suspect it? *Aasjäger*!!" But Preuss would have none of it and followed Udet back to his airfield:

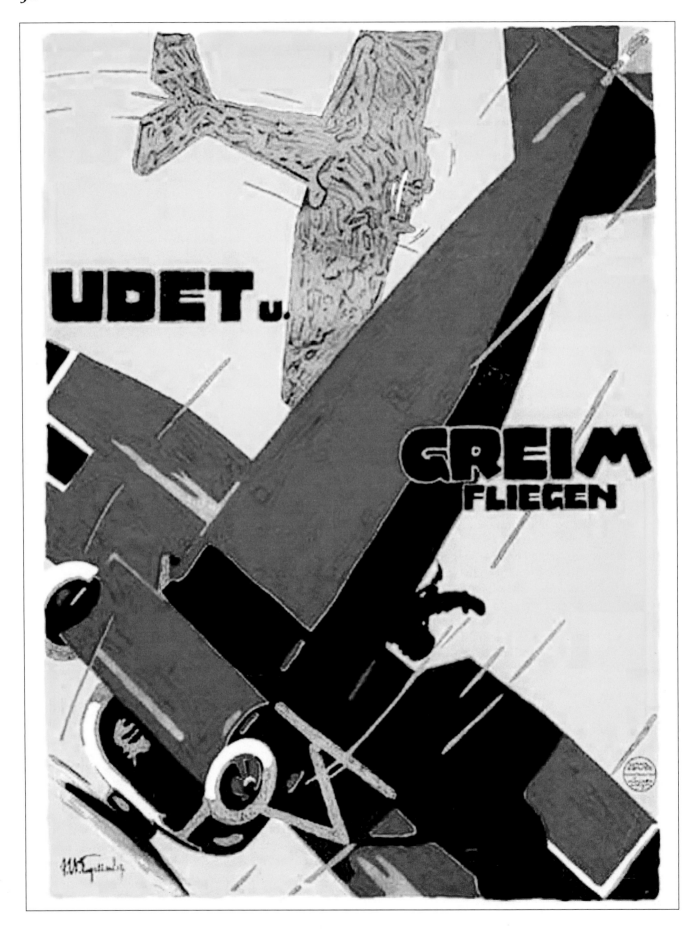

Above & Facing Page: Two posters advertising flying displays put on by Udet and Greim. (images courtesy of Greg VanWyngarden)

BAY. FLIEGERGEDENKTAGE
Hpt. HAILER OL. UDET v. RICHTHOFEN

Above & Facing Page: Udet attended the *Bayerische Fliegergedenktage* (Bavarian Aviator Commemoration Day) held in Munich in May 1921. In the first image, Udet is flanked by Lothar von Richthofen (left) and Franz Hailer (right). The man at far left may have been Friedrich Schubert. In the second, Udet (left foreground) and others watch an aerial display. The man at center (wearing a scarf and flight helmet) was Gustav *Ritter* von Kahr (Minister-President of Bavaria), and moving right from him were Franz Hailer (dark patch on collar) and Ernst Pöhner (Munich's Chief of Police). Udet had just taken Kahr and Pöhner up for a ride.

"We both jump out and he approaches me: 'You shot at me!' I am flabbergasted! I thought I had earned some thanks when I came to the aid of the red machine and now this is my reward. I am at a loss. 'I recognized your machine precisely,' Udet says in a calm but certain tone. Now it dawns on me. 'Did you recognize my [personal] insignia or just the colors of our *Staffel*?' He is the one who is astonished now. 'Were there more machines of your *Staffel* there?' 'Certainly!' 'Then it could have been someone else.'"

Preuss returned to his field and asked one of the members of his flight if he had fired on a red machine. The young airman, having heard stories of the red machines of French aces such as Jean Navarre and Georges Madon, had mistaken Udet for one of them. Preuss drove with the young man to Udet's airfield to apologize, but asked that Udet go easy on him: "Udet laughs. 'It's just a good thing

that you are such a bad marksman. Three times you fired from point blank range without inflicting a single hit upon me.'" Soon all was forgiven and Udet told Preuss he would make no claim on his Frenchman since Preuss had fired first. But artillery eyewitnesses on the ground later reported that Preuss and Udet had sent down both Frenchmen (the ones pursuing Udet) at the same time within 500 meters of one another – so their victories were indeed separate. Preuss wrote:

"I can inform Udet that our opponents are not identical, but rather that each of us had one. Only I cannot understand how Udet could renounce his claim so readily when he knew perfectly well that he had finished his off! Is such modesty not actually false? Only a man of Udet's stamp could act in such a way. I do not know whether there are many people like that."

Preuss visited his victim's crash site and discovered "a handsome little fellow with blond locks and well cared for hands." The dead man carried several newspaper clippings and citations on him, one of which noted that he was an ace who had been awarded the *Médaille Militaire*. When presented with this information, Greg VanWyngarden recalled that Walter Zuerl had cited Jacques Gérard as Preuss' third victory in his *Pour le mérite-Flieger*. Upon further investigation, it was determined that Gérard, an ace with eight victories, had been killed on 3 July and had indeed been awarded the *Médaille Militaire*. VanWyngarden contacted David Méchin for more details on Gérard and Méchin not only confirmed that Gérard's personnel file had described him as having "medium blond" hair but also provided two photographs of the airman. So there is little doubt that Gérard had been killed by Preuss and that Udet's victim had been Gérard's squadron mate, Georges Lienhard.[88]

Continuing the String

Shortly after his 40th victory, Udet was sent to Adlershof airfield, outside of Berlin, to participate in fighter aircraft evaluations that were held as an adjunct to the Second Fighter Competition of 27 May-28 June 1918.[89] From there, he went on to Munich where he dictated the contents of what would be published as *Kreuz wider Kokarde*. He returned to *Jasta* 4 just as the unit moved its airfield to Ferme de Puisieux, 5 kilometers northeast of Laon, and was back in the air on 1 August when he was credited with no less than three victories.

The first was over a Nieuport 28 from 27th Aero Squadron, USAS. Two flights from that unit were flying protection for a pair of Salmson 2A2s on a photographic mission when they ran into Fokker D.VII fighters from *Jastas* 4 and 6.[90] A series of dogfights ensued and five Americans were forced down in German territory by Udet, *Lt*. Johannes Jessen, *Lt*. Egon Koepsch (*Jasta* 4), *Lt*. Richard Wenzl, and *Lt*. Franz Hemer (*Jasta* 6).[91] The five 27th Aero pilots were 1Lt. Charles B. Sands, 1Lt. A.L. Whiton, 1Lt. R.C. Martin, 1Lt. J.S. Hunt, and 1Lt. Oliver T. Beauchamp. Sands was shot down in flames and most historians have ascribed his demise to Udet.

Udet's second victory of the day was a Breguet north of Muret-et-Crouttes at 12:15 German time. He wrote about this victory in "My Experiences with the BMW Motor Type IIIa," referred to above on page 55:

"On the 1st of August, 1918, I led *Jasta* 4 on a front patrol at 15,000 feet. About 5,000 feet above us a French reconnaissance machine was returning from German territory. When I first saw him he was about 2 miles behind our lines. I at once opened my throttle and climbed rapidly away from the rest of my *Staffel* in an attempt to prevent the enemy from crossing the lines. Since there was a strong west wind his progress towards the lines was slow. He must have seen me about this time, because he now turned away to the southwest. Although at first our distance apart was considerable, it began to decrease slowly. I looked at the altimeter and found that I was at 20,000 feet. When still about 600 yards away from him he started to circle, presumedly to escape my fire. I was not thinking about firing yet, however, and it pleased me that I was able to close rapidly. Shortly before attacking I looked for my *Staffel*, and they were far away and well below me. I was now at 20,500 feet and aiming at the Frenchman, opened fired at about 90 yards range. After the first few shots a cloud of white vapour issued from the enemy machine, a sure sign that I had hit his fuel tank. His motor also now seemed to be giving him some trouble, and after a few more shots at 50 yards he spun away into the depths. The strong west wind drifted him back behind our lines, and at 12:15 he hit the ground at Muret-et-Crouettes [*sic*] and the wreckage burst into flames. Nothing recognisable was left except the blackened number, B2710."[92]

The death certificates for *Spa* 62's *MdL.* André Gabriel Léopold LeBrun and *Lt.* Marie Robert Brumauld des Allées inform us that they were shot down and killed that day "at Muret-et-Crouttes near Chacrise (Aisne)." The only complication with identifying them as Udet's 42nd is that an extensive database of Breguet serial numbers maintained by French air historians tells us that LeBrun and Brumauld des Allées were flying Breguet XIV A.2 2752 – not 2710; however, a photo of Udet's postwar apartment displays the rudder fabric of Breguet XIV A.2 "275_" (the final number is not visible) on his wall, which seems to confirm that they were his victims and that "2710" was an error.[93]

The last of Udet's 'triple' occurred north of Beugneux at 8:30 p.m. (German time). Again, multiple candidates exist for this with no clear favorite.

Sgt. Gratien Auguste Henri Verrier of *Spa* 76, flying a SPAD XIII, went missing during a patrol on 4 August and never returned to base. Two years later, it was determined that he had been killed "in the region of Soissons." Udet claimed a SPAD south of "Braisne," which was actually Braine, 12 kilometers east of Soissons.[94] So Verrier might have been Udet's victim that day.

On 8 August, *JG* I was ordered to fly to an airfield outside of Péronne to help counter the British breakthrough at Villers-Bretonneux. From there, Udet scored another 'triple' that same day: two SE.5s and a Sopwith Camel whose serial number – D9841 – joined others that adorned his Berlin apartment's wall. Udet related the story of this fight to David B. Rogers, who translated it this way in "How I Shot Down 62 Planes – From the War Log of Ernst Udet" for the May 1931 edition of *Fawcett's Battle Stories*:

"It was nearly dark on the evening of August 8, 1918, that I was coasting along at an altitude of 2500 feet in my red Fokker, D-7 (4253), in escort with several other planes when an Englishman swooped in from an angle, the guns in his Camel chattering a death dirge for me. I banked up on one wing, circled up and gained the top position, re-attacking at once. The Englishman pushed his nose down and went into a screaming dive with me on his tail. He continued his mad dive down to 1000 feet when he suddenly pulled the nose up and came back at me in an Immelmann. I held my course, thinking that he would swerve off to one side and that I would get him as we passed. He kept right on coming. Apparently he had figured things out the same way I had. The situation immediately became a test of nerve. He wouldn't give in. Neither would I. We both started shooting as soon as our planes got within range of each other. But our shots all went wild. In a moment we were so close that we could shout to each other. I started to curse. I guess he did the same. We were a pair of stubborn, damn fools. The next moment the inevitable had happened. With a terrific crash, we came together. I was tossed into the cockpit by the impact. There was a jar, a jolt, a bump, a rending, tearing noise. The next thing I knew my machine had broken clear and when I looked back the Camel was falling earthward in a series of drunken curves. Having the top position and my speed being greater than his, I carried more potential destruction. My undercarriage struck the upper surface of his wings and crushed them. But that Englishman had grit. He manipulated his controls and got his machine straightened out. Then he broke into another spin. I thought it was all up with him because by that time he was pretty well down. But less than a hundred feet up he got her straightened out again and held her under partial control until he hit the ground in a cloud of dust. His plane was completely wrecked in landing."

The pilot, Lt. R.E. Taylor of RAF No.54 Squadron, survived and was taken prisoner.

Two Camels followed on 9 August before the *Geschwader* moved a little farther south on the 10th to a field straddling the road between Ennemain and Falvy. Udet added two more Camels to his victory log later that day, but suffered the loss of his good friend and chief rival for the title of Germany's highest-scoring living ace, *Oblt.* Erich Loewenhardt, the CO of *Jasta* 10.[95][96] Loewenhardt had 54 victories at the time of his death and Udet (62) and Manfred von Richthofen (80) were the only German pilots to surpass that total during the Great War. Duty was duty, and Udet scored another victory on

Left: Udet (in cockpit) and Thea Rasche, in flight gear just to the left of Udet, are besieged by photographers at 1928's *Volksflugtag* (People's Aviation Day) at Staaken. Rasche was Germany's first certified female aerobatics pilot. (photo courtesy of Greg VanWyngarden)

the 11th before *JG* I moved yet again to an airfield outside of Bernes on the 12th. Udet added to his tally from there on 12 and 14 August and then exceeded Loewenhardt's record by claiming his 55th on 15 August – a Sopwith Camel near Herleville. 1Lt. Lawrence T. Wyly of the 148th Aero Squadron, USAS, was wounded in combat and forced to land at the British trench map location "Sheet 66E.F.10A," a site that is about 5 kilometers south of Herleville. Wyly had claimed a Fokker D.VII within minutes of Udet's success.

After the war, the wall of Udet's Berlin apartment displayed the *Escadrille Spa 3* stork insignia that was cut from *Sous-Lt*. Jean Edouard Caël's SPAD XIII 4848 on 16 August 1918. The 5 February 1920 edition of *La Vie Aérienne* published Caël's account of the fight:

"It was the 16th of August 1918. While leading a patrol, I was abandoned by my comrades. Then I spotted above Foucaucourt a mêlée between 15 English planes and 17 Boches led by Lieutenant Udet. I rushed to the aid of the British. I arrived while being copiously fired upon from right and left. I brought down one of the enemies in flames—my fourth—and forced another one to go down. But it was a closely fought match and I couldn't even think about following his descent. A Sopwith single-seater was attacked by Udet from close quarters. I rushed over in an attempt to help him out. The poor Englishman appeared to be lost. He emitted a long white trail which soon became worrisome. I turned to extract him from the situation, and attacked the

German from the front at a three-quarters angle. Udet took up the challenge. The Sopwith availed himself of the opportunity to escape. And then began the duel between myself and the enemy ace of aces. It lasted a long time. We turned around each other, resorting to every sort of acrobatics. Neither of us was able to gain an advantage over the other. Then suddenly my propeller stopped, and I had to go into a nosedive. My adversary took advantage of this and stuck to my back like a leech. Coming about, I saw him quite clearly. I ducked my head down as his burst of fire passed over me. His bullets struck my right wing and the stabilizer. Then followed a second volley, and the latter gave way. The support strut flew off, taking with it the stabilizer. The tailplane was coming off. The situation was critical. This was even more true because Udet was closing in on me, giving the impression that a collision was imminent. When my stabilizer flew off, the shock was so great that I lost consciousness for a moment. That was in fact my salvation. Once I had seen what danger I was in, I had considered jumping overboard in order to make a speedy end of it. As it was, my airplane, which had fallen out of control, recovered. Then once more it went into a dive. Then it reared up, only to begin diving again. I did come to my senses. But then Udet was still there! I then landed, or rather I just plopped down. However, Udet was still pursuing me and kept firing on me even though I was on the ground. Later on I reproached him for this. He made some sort of excuse, saying that the lines were poorly defined and that he was afraid that I was going to escape. In order to avoid the bullets, I crawl under my plane. Finally, I use my engine as a sort of shield, and don't budge. Udet does not insist. Only an old reconnaissance plane comes by from time to time to take a crack at me. I try to lift my spirits. I am in fact in a bad spot. I'll try to hide in a dugout where I'll keep a look-out. I am roused by a Boche patrol firing off some shots from their rifles close to my ears in order to revive me: funny way to go about it! They take me to a trench, where they make me drink some unspeakable wine in order to restore my strength."[97]

Caël said that Udet visited him afterward and when they were alone, assured Caël that he was not there to interrogate him but only to see about his wellbeing. In fact, Udet not only did not ask any questions of Caël but instead told him about some interesting things. For example, Udet described the parachutes that German pilots were using and said that he had had to use one twice. Udet also told Caël that his favorite apparatus for traveling back to Germany was a 140-hp SPAD. At the end of the visit, Udet hesitatingly signaled that he wanted to shake hands and Caël took him up on it. In closing, Caël asserted that Udet was the most proper German he had ever encountered and seemed to be "a bit of a surprise among the Boches."

We have photographic evidence that might support Udet's having used a captured SPAD to travel in German territory (see p.141 below), but we know of only one instance where Udet had to take to his parachute (see above, p.54).

Udet was awarded a 'double" on 21 August. The first of them involved an SE.5 south of Hébuterne at 5:30 p.m. (English time), but it has not yet been identified.[98] The second was a Camel near Courcelles-le-Comte, and several historians have identified the 148th Aero Squadron's 2Lt. T.W. Imes, who was wounded in action and crashed west of Mercatel, as his victim. The identification has been tentative, however, because it was noted that Udet's claim took place at 6:15 p.m. whereas Imes was reported as having started his patrol at 6:45 p.m.

Another 'double' followed the next day on 22 August. The first was Sopwith Camel F1969 from No.80 Squadron, RAF. The encounter with his second began when a telephone call reported that two German balloons had just been shot down by an enemy squadron:

"We take off at once, the entire *Jasta* 4 with all available machines, toward Braie [Bray-sur-Somme]. We're flying at three thousand meters altitude, the chain of German balloons below us, obliquely above us the British squadron, five SE.5s. We stay below

them and wait for their attack...Suddenly, like an arrow, a machine darts down past me toward the balloons. I push down behind him. It's one of the English squadron, their leader. The narrow streamer flutters in front of me. I push down, down, down. The air screams at the windshield. I have to reach him, catch up, stop him from getting to the balloons. Too late! The shadow of his apparatus flits across the taut skin of the balloon like a fish in shallow water...a small blue flame flares up, creeps slowly over its gray back, and the next moment a column of fire shoots up toward the heavens where, just a moment ago, the golden yellow bag had floated with a silken glow...A very tight turn; the Englishman goes down almost perpendicularly, the troops at the balloon cable winch scatter. But the SE.5 has already flattened out and is sweeping westward, close to the ground – so close to the ground that the machine and its shadow merge into one. But now I am behind him. A wild chase begins, barely three meters above the earth. We jump over telegraph poles, over roadside trees. A mighty leap, the church steeple of Marécourt [sic – Maricourt]. But I stay behind him and can't be shaken off. The army road to Arras. Flanked by tall trees, it winds through the landscape like a green wall. He flies to the right of the row of trees, I to the left. I fire every time there is a gap in the treetops. Alongside the road, on a meadow, German infantry are encamped. Even though I am right on his neck, he fires at them. But that is his undoing. At the same moment I jump over the treetops – hardly 10 meters separate us – and fire. A tremor runs through his machine; the airplane wavers, staggers in a turn, hits the ground, bounces up again like a stone skipping water, and disappears in a mighty leap behind a small birch grove. A cloud of dust rises up. Sweat is running down my face in streams, fogs my goggles, gums up my eyes. I wipe my forehead with my jacket sleeve. It is midsummer, 22 August, 12:30 p.m., the hottest day of the year..."[99]

The daring pilot was the renowned Irish ace Capt. Tom Falcon Hazell of No.40 Squadron, who actually made it back to his base at Bertangles. His report stated that he had attacked a balloon at Maricourt at 11:20 a.m. (12:20 p.m. German time), shot it down, and then "was seen home by the E[nemy] A[ircraft], who shot his tank, longerons and propeller to pieces."[100] His SE.5a B8422.B was so badly shot up that it was written off as not worth repairing.

An exhausted Udet began four weeks of leave on 22 August, but not before briefly meeting with *JG* I's commander, *Oblt.* Hermann Göring. When Göring had first arrived at *JG* I on 14 July 1918 and then gone on a five-week leave of his own on 26 July, Udet had been back in Germany. Göring's first day back on the job was on 22 August, just as Udet was departing; so this probably was their first introduction to one another. Little did either man suspect that it was the beginning of an association that would culminate in Udet's death in 1941.

When Udet returned to duty on 25 September, *JG* I had been moved to Metz. From there, Udet achieved his final two successes of the war on 26 September. He recounted:

"Shellbursts on the horizon, little black clouds of German flak, enemy aircraft in sight. They come closer, seven machines, de Havilland 9 two-seaters. We are six. But the ones out there are new at the front, an American formation. The youngest of us have two years of combat experience behind them. We meet close to the airfield. The whole thing lasts hardly five minutes. Gluczewski brings one down, Kraut too; mine comes down in flames near Monteningen [Montigny-lès-Metz]. The others turn around and fly home. One individual brushes past just above me. I put my Fokker on its tail and fire straight up into the air. He can no longer avoid me and must pass through my burst of fire. He explodes just barely fifty meters above me, and I have to dive away fast to avoid being hit by the burning debris."[101]

Udet's original combat report for the last of these stated:

"After shooting down the first D.H.9, I again attacked the formation which now consisted of only 5 or 4 elements on their return flight. I shot the middle D.H.9 which first began to 'stink' [i.e., smoke] and then burned right afterward. The flames decreased somewhat and flared up again. The crash occurred in the region south of Metz."[102]

A large formation of DH.9s from No.99 Squadron (Independent Force) had tried to reach Thionville but had to drop their bombs on Metz instead. On their way back, they were attacked by airmen from *Jastas* 3, 4, 15, and 77. Seven of them were shot down or forced to land so it is difficult to tell which two might have been Udet's final victories of the war. One of the 99 Squadron aircraft exacted a modicum of revenge on Udet, however:

"A third whips past me toward the west. The leader's streamer flutters on his tail. I go behind him. When he realizes that he is being followed, he turns around and flies at me. A salvo bursts out from over there; I feel a burning pain in my left thigh, and gasoline comes spurting out of my holed tank like a shower. I cut the ignition and land...I climb out of the plane and have a look at my wound. The shot went through the thick flesh and a bit of blood still oozes out. The others step aside, and Göring comes up to me. I report: '61st and 62nd opponents shot down. Myself slightly wounded. Shot through the left buttock, face undamaged.' Göring laughs and shakes my hand."[103]

Udet went to a nearby field hospital for treatment and returned to *JG* I on 3 October. His war flying days were essentially over, however, and on 11 October he was transferred to *FEA* 3 at Gotha. He was subsequently sent to Mannheim to visit the Rhemag-Rhenania Motor Factory and then attended the Third Fighter Competition held at Adlershof from 10 to 28 October. The Great War ended soon afterward on 11 November 1918 and Udet went back home to Munich.

Postwar

Udet was released from military service on 10 January 1919, after which he was employed in the automobile division of the Gustav Otto Werke. He desperately wanted to fly again, however, and made plans with another wartime ace, Robert *Ritter* von Greim, to conduct airshows for the public; but aircraft proved difficult to come by for civilians. Moreover, their hopes received a severe blow on 28 June 1919 when Germany signed the Versailles Treaty temporarily forbidding the manufacture and importation of aircraft in Germany and requiring the surrender of all existing military aircraft to the Allies within three months. When the men discovered that several Fokker D.VIIs and D.VIIIs had been taken to Bamberg to await delivery to the Allies, they resourcefully convinced the aircraft's keepers to lend them a few for shows to benefit German prisoners of war. Udet also obtained a new Pfalz D.XV from the closed factory at Speyer, whose owners were probably all too happy to keep it out of Allied hands.[104]

Udet and Greim subsequently put on shows at Munich's Oberwiesenfeld airfield on 11 August and over Tegernsee Lake on 21 August. Greim's aircraft touched a power line and crashed into the lake during the latter, however, and although he escaped without serious injury, their enterprise came to a halt. Both men then found employment with the Bayerische Rumpler-Werke (Bavarian Rumpler Works) in September 1919 and flew Rumpler aircraft in various airshows.

All of this came to a halt on 10 January 1920 when the Versailles Treaty took effect and Udet and Greim could no longer fly their aircraft. Some of the restrictions imposed by the treaty were relaxed the following September, and the Rumpler Company took advantage of the respite to try to launch Germany's first international airline. Udet, who had married his long-time girlfriend, Eleonore "Lo" Zink, on 25 February 1920, took her on the maiden flight from Munich to Vienna that he piloted on 20 October. Upon landing, however, the airplane was promptly impounded by Allied authorities who claimed that they had not authorized the flight. Udet found himself grounded once again and he and his wife had to return to Munich by train.

Munich native Heinz Pohl and his brother Wilhelm, who had moved to Milwaukee, Wisconsin, believed that there was a market for German-made light aircraft in Germany and the United States. They also believed that the Versailles Treaty provisions that banned such an activity would be lifted in the near future. The name "Udet" would have great value in such a market, so they proposed a joint venture with him that he accepted in late 1921. At first, their aircraft were secretly produced in a small workshop at Milbertshofen, next door to Oberwiesenfeld; but when the Allied Control Commission became aware of its existence, the shop was moved to Ramersdorf. But then the wraps were taken off when the Allies lifted the ban on German aircraft manufacturing on 5 May 1922. Shortly afterwards on 16 May, Udet made a successful test flight of their first design, the U-1. As a result, Udet, Heinz Pohl, and two others publicly registered Udet Flugzeugbau (Udet Aircraft Manufacturing) on 23 October 1922 and went about developing their next design, the U-2.

Things were going well for the business but not for his marriage. Udet, an inveterate partier and womanizer, was not suited for conventional marriage and the couple were divorced on 16 February 1923, just nine days shy of their third wedding anniversary. Their split was relatively amicable, however, and they maintained contact throughout the years that followed.

The notion of selling his aircraft in the United States never materialized, so Udet traveled to Argentina in April 1923 to demonstrate and market his designs in South America. This was followed by similar efforts in Europe after Bäumer-Aero, the company founded by the well-known German ace, Paul Bäumer, obtained the sales rights for Udet Flugzeugbau's aircraft. New designs, designated U-4 through U-12, were rolled out and the firm became a lucrative concern. Udet, never an avid businessman and more interested in flying, sold his interest in the company in 1925 but continued to receive royalties on sales of his designs.

Udet augmented his income by flying in airshows, competitions, and corporate publicity flights across Germany and other European countries. He was a stunt flier par excellence and was known for such daring feats as picking up a handkerchief from the ground with his airplane's wingtip, looping within feet of the ground, or landing on an exact spot following a sideslipping, deadstick descent. He soon became a celebrity throughout the continent and was even feted by his former enemies, the French, in 1926. Udet moved to Berlin in 1927 and continued both his flying activities and a lavish lifestyle that often left him broke. So he began searching for other sources of revenue. Udet had been a gifted illustrationist since his childhood and in 1928 he published a collection of amusing, aviation-themed cartoons that was titled *Hals und Beinbruch* – the phrase German aviators had used to wish each other luck during the war.[105]

He played roles in and performed flying stunts for the movies *Die weisse Hölle vom Piz Palü* (*The White Hell of Piz Palü*) in 1929, *Stürme über dem Mont Blanc* (*Storms Over Mont Blanc*) and *Fremde Vögel über Afrika* (*Strange Birds Over Africa*) in 1930, and .*O.S. Eisberg* (*S.O.S. Iceberg*) in 1932, and *Wunder des Fliegens* (*The Miracle of Flying*) in 1935. While doing so, he traveled to such far-flung parts of the world as Greenland and Africa. He participated in flight competitions held in France, Great Britain, and the United States, where he met up with the great French ace, René Fonck, America's Ace of Aces, Eddie Rickenbacker, and Walter Wanamaker – the man he had downed for his 39th victory. The two men had corresponded after the war, and during a visit to the United States on 6 September 1931, they met in person again during a Cleveland Airshow. When Wanamaker began to deliver a prepared speech for the crowd, Udet surprised him by producing the piece of fabric he had cut from his machine and made a gift of it to him, saying "I now give you what I took away."[106] Wanamaker spontaneously invited Udet to have dinner with him at his home in Akron, which Udet happily accepted, and the former foes chatted and drank wine together well into the evening. On a subsequent trip to the United States, he was entertained by some of Hollywood's biggest stars including Mary Pickford, Lilian Harvey, and Harold Lloyd.

Herman Göring, now a prominent, high-ranking figure in the German government following Adolf Hitler's appointment as chancellor on January 1933, recognized that Udet's celebrity status could be of great value to the Nazi Party as well as to him personally and his efforts to rebuild the German Air Force. He had already approached Udet once about joining forces but had been rebuffed with the statement: "Politics don't interest me. They are just a noise in the background."[107] Later, Göring learned that during Udet's visit to the United States in 1931, he had been greatly impressed by the Curtiss-Wright Company's line of aircraft – particularly its F6C Hawk fighter. In fact, he had wanted to purchase one of the fighters but found that he could not raise the necessary funds. So, just before Udet's second trip to the U.S. in 1933, Göring arranged another meeting with him where he once again invited Udet to join the cause. This time, however, he added irresistible inducement:

"To show you that I want to help you I'll give you the dollars you need to buy a Curtiss Hawk. In fact, you'll buy two Hawks. I'm curious to know what they can do and want them thoroughly tested at Rechlin; after which they'll be yours to do whatever you like with them."[108]

Udet accepted the offer and in return, joined the Nazi Party on 1 May 1933. He then traveled to the United States, purchased two Curtiss Hawks, and arranged for their transport to Germany. After their arrival, he demonstrated them for high-ranking

Reichsluftfahrtministerium (German Aviation Ministry, or *RLM*) officials and was subsequently asked by one of them, Erhard Milch, to attend all future *RLM* conferences concerning such aircraft. Udet was slowly being drawn into military circles again. Consequently, after the Luftwaffe was officially formed as a separate arm of the German military on 26 February 1935, Udet entered it as an *Oberst* on 18 May with an effective date of 1 June.

On 1 September 1935, Udet was assigned to Hermann Göring's *Reichsluftfahrtministrium*. Göring continued to push Udet into key administrative roles and despite Udet's protestations, named him *Chef des Technischen Amtes* (Chief of the Technical Office) on 10 June 1936, the position that was responsible for overseeing all of the Luftwaffe's research, development, and supply programs. General Alfred Mahncke, a veteran aviator of the First World War who also rose to high-ranking positions in the Luftwaffe, wrote:

"With this appointment, one of the most famous German fighter pilots took the stage. He was a close friend of Göring and extremely popular, but six years later he departed as a tragic character...I have never understood how he, an endearing man and a likeable comrade, could be pushed into this important post, which he had attempted to refuse to accept because he knew his strong and weak points only too well. For anyone acquainted with aviation, it was clear that the office of Chief of the Technical Office would one day hold the key to victory or defeat for the Luftwaffe in battle. It was a post requiring technical and organizational abilities of the highest order, an almost superhuman capacity for hard work and great resolve. The appointee also had to be ruthless towards meddlers. Udet was the typical, easy-going fighter ace – a reliable friend, sensitive and easily influenced. He had lots of charm and possessed an artist's eye, and with pencil and brush produced exquisite, witty and humorous caricatures of people and situations – himself included. But first and foremost he was a wonderfully gifted pilot with a sixth sense, an aerobatic artist of the highest order. He was a Bohemian and enjoyed the company of artists, actors, and painters, preferring their companionship to that of soldiers, and it must be said in his favour that he was reluctant to become a soldier again. But Göring overrode his reservations, appealed to his friendship, and eventually made him into someone he never wanted to be."[109]

Udet played a key role in the evolution of such famous aircraft as the Junkers Ju 87 and 88, Heinkel He 111, Messerschmidt Bf 109 and 110, Dornier Do 17, and Focke-Wulf Fw 190, and rose through the ranks from *Oberstleutnant* to *Generaloberst*. But he was neither a good administrator nor a good politician, and the intrigues, dishonesty, and power grabs of his fellow Nazi officials eventually overwhelmed him. Moreover, as the war progressed and it became clear that German aircraft development and production could not keep pace with the war's needs, many of those officials including Hermann Göring made Udet – who had predicted this outcome – the scapegoat for their failures. George C. Monkhouse, a British engineer, photographer, and racing enthusiast recalled Udet as being extremely disillusioned with Germany's state of affairs as early as the summer of 1939, when he was invited to a dinner that Udet had organized:

"Practically at 12 o'clock, then, we stopped fishing and made our way up to the Haus Buchenbichl, there to find General Udet...He then went on to say how nice it was to meet us, and that he had arranged with Herr Popp that the four of us had dinner that night, and he would tell us all about Hitler, who he said was a stark lunatic, Goering, Goebbels and the rest of the German hierarchy. Popp had taken the precaution of sending Erica and her mother out for the evening as well as the servants. They had cooked the dinner, and it was only necessary for us to get it out of the oven. Before starting the meal, however, Udet and Popp took all the curtains down, the carpets up, the cushions out of the furniture, the pictures off the wall, and generally inspected the premises for 'bugging,' as this was a favourite trick of the Gestapo if they suspected something. Finding nothing, we then sat down to a meal...All this was consumed together with multitudinous bottles of Rhine wine, and then we got down to talk. Udet showed no hesitation in telling us in no uncertain terms the ridiculous situation in Germany, with all these madmen trying to run their affairs. He went on to say that if Germany could win the war in a week or so, that would be one thing, but he thought this would be quite impossible, and that it would only be a matter of time before America came into the conflict, and then that would be the end of things for Germany – and anyone who thought otherwise had taken leave of their senses!"[110]

Udet became increasingly depressed and turned to alcohol and drugs for relief. His health deteriorated and he began to speak of suicide to his closest friends after Hitler attacked the Soviet Union in 21 June 1941. On 16 November, Udet and his girlfriend, Inge Bleyle, had dinner with some good friends. Udet drank cognac throughout the evening and

Above & Right: Udet met two of his American opponents at the Cleveland Air Show of 1931. Here we see him as he met with Edward "Eddie" Rickenbacker and then later with his 39th victim, Walter Wanamaker. Udet returned the serial number that he had removed from Wanamaker's machine back on 2 July 1918.

continued doing so after he had dropped her off at her apartment. Early the next morning, he called Inge, who asked if he had slept well. His response was "No!" and when she said that she was coming over for breakfast, he said: "No, don't come. It's too late. Ingelein, nobody was dearer to me than you." He then placed his Colt handgun to his right temple and pulled the trigger while she was still on the line. He had left a suicide note that included the message: "Iron One, you are responsible for my death."

Above: Udet was famous for a stunt where he used his wingtip to pick up a handerkerchief from the ground. Here we see him holding that handkerchief while conversing with someone.

Facing Page: This is the Curtiss Hawk II that Udet flew in an aerobatics display for the 1936 Olympic Games held in Berlin. It is now on display at the *Muzeum Lotnictwa Polskiego w Krakowie* (Polish Aviation Museum in Krakow). (photos courtesy of Colin Owers and Piotr Mrozowski)

Above: A postwar portrait of Udet.

The Nazis could not stand to have it known that one of Germany's best-known heroes had killed himself because of them; so they told the public that Udet had died in a tragic flying accident and gave him a state funeral on 22 November. The man who presided over that funeral and delivered Udet's eulogy was "The Iron One" himself – Hermann Göring. Udet was placed in a grave at Berlin's Invalidenfriedhof cemetery where many of Germany's military heroes had been interred; but after the Soviets took over that part of the city in 1945, his headstone was removed. Following the fall of the Berlin Wall, however, a new marker was erected at his gravesite that can be viewed today.

Endnotes

[1] *Kreuz wider Kokarde*, p.12.
[2] Ibid., p.13. When Udet was serving in the Alsace region with *Artillerie-Flieger-Abteilung* (*AFA*) 206, his small stature earned him the Alsatian nickname 'Kneckes,' (British 'Titch' or American 'Shorty'). Udet transcribed this as 'Knägges.'
[3] Ibid.
[4] Ibid., p.15.
[5] Ibid., pp.15-16.
[6] *Mein Fliegerleben*, p.10.
[7] *Kreuz wider Kokarde*, p.21. "Twice sewn holds better" is the equivalent of "better safe than sorry."
[8] His observer on the last of the tests – the *Flugmeister-Prüfung* (Flight Master Examination) – was a "*Lt.* Gerlich" who may have been Martin Gerlich. Gerlich joined *Kampfgeschwader* 1 in February 1916 and was credited with four victories by the following August and was featured on a Sanke postcard as a result. He later became the adjutant for *Kampfgeschwader* 3, serving under Ernst Brandenburg and Rudolf Kleine (see Bronnenkant, *The Imperial German Eagles in World War I*, Vol.1, pp.138-40.
[9] Although Udet spoke of Justinus in *Kreuz wider Kokarde* and *Mein Fliegerleben*, *Ace of the Iron Cross* mistakenly refers to him as "Justinius."
[10] Justinus was raised to *Oberleutant* and became a pilot himself before serving with *Jagdstaffel* (*Jasta*) 35b in September 1917. He was the unit's acting CO when he was shot down and killed on 30 January 1918.
[11] *Mein Fliegerleben*, p.14.
[12] Ibid.
[13] Ibid., p.15.
[14] *Kreuz wider Kokarde*, p.35.
[15] *AFP* Gaede's airfield was only a short distance away to the northeast outside of Biesheim.
[16] *Mein Fliegerleben*, p.27.
[17] This was the story presented in *Mein Fliegerleben* (pp.30–31), which was supported by a photograph of the cockpit displaying the tangled cable. *Kreuz wider Kokarde* (p.36) was different, however, in that it placed the blame on the aircraft having "tightened up during a long stand in the rain." Evidently, the wartime publishers (or military censors) did not want to admit to any design or manufacturing defect.
[18] *Main Fliegerleben*, pp.33-35. *Kreuz wider Kokarde* (pp.36–37) differed by stating that he had fired at a Voisin biplane from 600 meters away – too great a distance – and that neither of them scored a hit. We can surmise that the wartime publication could not have a German fighter pilot and hero admitting that he had lost his nerve during combat.
[19] Pfältzer may have put in a claim for a Farman that was subsequently believed to have collided with an AEG from *FFA* 48, killing both crews. *FFA* 48 was also based at Habsheim.
[20] *Kreuz wider Kokarde*, p.39.
[21] Ibid., p.42.

[22] *Mein Fliegerleben* jumps even further ahead to April 1917 and Udet's fifth victory.

[23] Udet's service record states that he was officially placed on *Jasta* 15's roster on 8 October 1916.

[24] *Kreuz wider Kokarde*, pp.45-46. *Fw.* Gustav Bauer of *FFA* 9b kept a photo of the captured Breguet with him standing in front of it in his personal album and labeled it: *"Luftkampf am 12.10.16 bei Colmar, abgeschossen von Feldwebel G. Bauer"* ("Air combat on 12 October 1916 by Colmar, shot down by *Feldwebel* G. Bauer" (see *Das Propellerblatt* 12, p.401). Evidently, he believed he had been the victor.

[25] See O'Connor, *Aviation Awards of Imperial Germany in World War I*, Vol.4, p.213.

[26] *Kreuz wider Kokarde*, pp.49-50.

[27] Ibid., pp.54-55.

[28] VanWyngarden, *Albatros Aces of World War 1*, Part 2, p.22.

[29] *Mein Fliegerleben*, p.46.

[30] This finds further support in the fact that the 5 and 10 May victories of *Jasta* 15's CO, *Lt.* Heinrich Gontermann, were near Craonne and Berry-au-Bac, which lay on either side of La Ville-aux-Bois-lès-Pontavert. Incidentally, Gontermann downed a SPAD VII from *Esc. N* 3 on 10 May.

[31] My thanks to David Méchin and Greg VanWyngarden for a copy of the *N* 3 logbook page. *Jasta* 1's *Lt.* Werner Zech has also been mentioned as Heurtaux's possible victor; but Zech's claim came at 11:05 a.m. – hours after Heurtaux had returned to his base.

[32] During their brief time together, Udet learned to greatly respect Gontermann and had several interesting things to say about him in *Mein Fliegerleben* (pp.48-51, 60-62). Alternatively, see Volume 8 of this series, pp.15-18.

[33] In a letter home, Gontermann related that five pilots had been killed (we know of only four) and another three sent home because of nervous breakdowns. See Müller, *Fliegerleutnant Heinrich Gontermann*, p.96. Just prior to Gontermann's arrival, one of Udet's closest friends, *Lt.* Hans-Olaf Esser, had been killed in action on 16 April.

[34] *Mein Fliegerleben*, p.57.

[35] The full inscription would have been *"Vieux Charles."*

[36] *Mein Fliegerleben*, pp.58–60. With the war still raging when it was published in 1918, it is no surprise that this marvelous act of chivalry by a Frenchman gained no mention in *Kreuz wider Kokarde*.

[37] *Kreuz wider Kokarde*, pp.67-68. My thanks to a discussion on the Rise of Flight website (https://riseofflight.com/forum/topic/29983-udet-vs-guynemer-fight-never-happened/) and to Greg VanWyngarden for mentioning it and other key pieces of information regarding Udet's claimed encounter with Guynemer.

[38] Page 1435. *Jasta* 16 pilot Max Holtzem told historian George Shiras "Lothar von Richthofen once recounted how a British opponent stopped his attack when he realized Lothar's guns were jammed." See *Cross & Cockade* 5:4, p.333.

[39] Binot, *Georges Guynemer*, pp.343-44. We do not know if Udet used the phrase *"un embryon de combat"* or if it was his interviewer's translation, but it seems to have meant something along the lines of only the beginning of a fight that did not fully develop. Udet also mentioned during the interview that the incident occurred in 1915 – not 1917. Was this just an innocent mistake or is it another sign that the incident was embellished or even fabricated?

[40] *Kreuz wider Kokarde*, pp.76-77.

[41] Since he landed right next to the airplane and it was taken into custody, it seems highly unlikely that he would have mistaken its type; besides, his next single-seat victory did not occur until 17 September and he not only retained a photo of it (a DH.5) but the pilot was also killed.

[42] Henshaw, *The Sky Their Battlefield II*, p.109.

[43] See Schmäling and Bock, *Royal Prussian Jagdstaffel 30*, p.60. Also, the *Armeeoberkommando (AOK)* 6 report for 12 August 1917 recorded an airplane *"bei Courrieres von Lt. Udet abgesch."* ("shot down by *Lt.* Udet at Courrieres"); but it was not officially awarded to him. I am indebted to Rainer Absmeier for providing copies of the *AOK* 6 reports cited herein.

[44] *Kreuz wider Kokarde*, pp.77-79.

[45] Udet originally believed it to have been a Martinsyde G.100 (again similar in appearnace to a DH.4) when he put in his claim, but evidently changed his mind in 1918. Obviously, in the heat of battle and following an explosion, he was never able to identify his victim's precise type. The *AOK* 6 report for the day was similarly confused, noting that *"1 Martinsyde durch Albatros über Pont à Vendin abgesch."* ("1 Martinsyde shot down by an Albatros over Pont-à-Vendin") and *"bei Annay abgestürzte Sopwith ist von Lt. Brügmann abgesch."* ("A Sopwith shot down by *Lt.* Brügmann crashed near Annay.") No Sopwith was lost that day anywhere in the vicinity.

[46] *Kreuz wider Kokarde*, pp.79-81.

[47] Ibid., pp.81-84.

[48] Ibid., pp.142-44.

[49] *Over the Front* 18:3, p.258.

[50] Ibid.

[51] See the footnote on p.48 of Ishoven, *The Fall of an Eagle: The Life of Fighter Ace Ernst Udet.*

[52] *Kreuz wider Kokarde*, pp.88-89.

[53] Gilbert was an Australian and a chapter in *Kreuz wider Kokarde* was devoted to *"Der letzte Kampf des australischen Leutnants"* ("The Australian 2nd Lieutenant's Final Battle") who flew a Sopwith Camel. Thus there has been some thought that the chapter described his fight with Gilbert – the discrepancy between a Camel and an SE.5a notwithstanding. Yet the chapter mentions Udet and his companions' "red aircraft," the German Fokker Triplane, and the fact that he had closely inspected the Australian 2nd Lieutenant's downed aircraft. So it would seem that the incident related in the chapter came after Udet had joined *Jasta* 11. In addition, the fact that he had seen his victim's aircraft close up makes it very unlikely that he would have mistaken an SE.5a for a Camel. None of the pilots Udet shot down while with *Jasta* 11 appears to have been Australian.

[54] *Kreuz wider Kokarde*, pp.90-91.

[55] Ibid., p.91.

[56] Ibid. Buckler had shot down five airplanes between 29 September and 17 October, bringing his total up to 18 confirmed victories – five more than Udet.

[57] Ibid., pp.91-95. Buckler, in his 1939 autobiography, *Malaula! Der Schlachtruf meiner Staffel*, pp.150-51 (see also the 2007 English translation edited by Norman Franks: *Malaula! The Battle Cry of Jasta 17*, pp.126-28) mentioned this meeting with Udet but his version was different. For example, he said that it had occurred right after his 16th victory and one of Udet's just minutes before; but Buckler's 16th fell on 11 October and Udet made no claim that day (in fact, the two men never did share victories on the same date). Buckler also said they had breakfast together – not lunch – after which they took off together, Buckler heading to his squadron and Udet to the front. Buckler then saw Udet being attacked and taking to his parachute – something Udet and all other German fighter pilots did not have at their disposal until well into 1918. These kinds of inaccuracies were common in Buckler's book, and since his recollection came some 21 years after Udet's, Udet's version is almost certainly more reliable. Unfortunately, Armand van Ishoven (*The Fall of an Eagle: The Life of Fighter Ace Ernst Udet*, pp.50–51) appears to have tried to reconcile both versions in 1977 and in the course of doing so introduced erroneous information of his own, such as the meeting occuring on 1 October (neither Buckler nor Udet scored a victory that day), Buckler's base being situated at Ghistelles (Gistel, Belgium) when it was at Wasquehal, and Udet coming down in the "flooded region around Nieuport and Dixmuiden." Neither Buckler nor Udet mentioned these things in their accounts.

[58] *Kreuz wider Kokarde*, pp.121-23. Udet did bring down a Sopwith Camel on 5 December, but it was in the afternoon (1:30 p.m. British time) and not the morning. Moreover, it was his 16th victory and not his particularly significant 20th.

[59] Ibid., p.131.

[60] My thanks to Greg VanWyngarden for bringing this article to my attention and to Adam Wait for his translation of it. The Triplanes' "long pause" had been in November 1917 when they were grounded pending an investigation into upper wing failures. They were allowed back in the air in December

[61] *Mein Fliegerleben*, p.65.

[62] *Kreuz wider Kokarde*, pp.131-32.

[63] *Mein Fliegerleben*, pp.67-68.

[64] Other candidates have been offered for Udet's 27 March victory (e.g. AW FK.8 B5828 or C3630) but they too involved crewmen who made it back alive.

[65] *Mein Fliegerleben*, pp.75–78. Udet was obviously confused regarding Maasdorp's country of origin. Here, he lists him as Canadian; but he may have been mixing Maasdorp up with his 47th victory, 2Lt. R.E. Taylor, whose calling card (souvenired by Udet) gave his address as "South Woodslee, Ontario." Udet gave almost the same account of this action in a chapter incorrectly titled *"Der letzte Kampf des australischen Leutnants"* ("The Australian 2nd Lieutenant's Last Battle") in *Kreuz wider Kokarde*, pp.155-57. Maasdorp was actually from Graaff-Reinet, South Africa. His mother, Molly, wrote Udet after the war and he sent her the pilot's license he had removed from her son's body.

[66] Bodenschatz, *Jagd in Flandern's Himmel*, p.175.

[67] Wenzl, *Richthofen-Flieger*, p.18.

[68] *Mein Fliegerleben*, pp.90–91. Udet's sister Irene had been born in 1908.

[69] Ibid., p.91.

[70] In *Mein Fliegerleben*, p. 91, Udet recalled that the jeweler was situated on Theatinerstrasse. Gebrüder Hemmerle (Hemmerle Brothers) was actually just around the corner at Maximilianstrasse 14 where it still operates today. Interestingly, Udet returned to the jewelry store in 1928 after he had lost his *Pour le Mérite*

while visiting the Zugspitzplateau region along the border between Bavaria and Austria. A surviving letter from Gebrüder Hemmerle tells us what happened: "20 March 1928. Dear Udet! In the spring of 1918 you stood in our shop and asked for a *Pour le Mérite*, which we unfortunately did not have in stock. Today, ten years later almost to the day, the same story! We can only help you out with our display model so that you don't have to search for your lost *P.l.M.* in the deep snow of the Zugspitzplateau." The display model and its accompanying letter were auctioned off in 2006.

[71] Ibid., pp.91-92. Shortly after returning to the front, Wenninger and a portion of his crew were captured by the British after their submarine struck a mine and sank on 22 April 1918 – the same day as Wenninger's 28th birthday.

[72] Ibid., pp.93.

[73] See Bodenschatz, *Jagd in Flanderns Himmel*, p.178 and O'Connor, *Aviation Awards of Imperial Germany in World War I*, Vol.4, p.213.

[74] The exhibition featured captured aircraft, aircraft flown by German heroes, and aviation-related military memorabilia. It closed in Munich on 16 June and went to Dortmund.

[75] *Mein Fliegerleben*, p.94.

[76] Udet said that upon his return, he visited the grave of *Lt.* Joachim Wolff, who had been killed on 16 May 1918.

[77] Béranger's certificate gives his date of death as 1 June 1918, but other records tell us he and Wolf were lost on 31 May; moreover, the other three men's certificates state 31 May 1918. If it was not simply a clerical error, perhaps Béranger died of his injuries on 1 June.

[78] *Lt.* Hans Kirschstein and *Lt.* Johann Janzen from *Jasta* 6 downed two SPADs around the same time near Villemontoire and Vierzy, but it has been offered elsewhere that their victims came from *Spa* 163 (*Cpl.* Marcel Girardeau and (Pierre?) Marsaux).

[79] *Kreuz wider Kokarde*, pp.170–71.

[80] Ibid., pp.165–67.

[81] *Memoirs of the Harvard Dead in the War Against Germany*, Vol.3, pp.342–43.

[82] *Kreuz wider Kokarde*, pp.179–84 and *Mein Fliegerleben*, pp.99–104.

[83] *Jagd in Flanderns Himmel*, pp.110–11.

[84] See *Cross & Cockade* 2:2, pp.97–99.

[85] *Kreuz wider Kokarde*, pp.174–76.

[86] *Popular Aviation* (Nov. 1931), p.15.

[87] Franks, Bailey, and Duiven, *The Jasta War Chronology*, p.200, gives the name as "Dompierre." Just five minutes before his SPAD victory, however, Drekmann had intercepted a Breguet from *Br* 128 that had been sent out to bomb Blérancourt and shot it down northwest of Nouvron[-Vingré]. There is no Dompierre anywhere near five minutes flying distance from this location, and Drekmann was flying a patrol with Udet when he downed his SPAD east of Laversine (9 km. south of Nouvron-Vingré). Accordingly, this must have been an error for Dommiers.

[88] For this entire story, including Wait's complete translation of Preuss' article, see *Over the Front* 29:3, pp.222–33.

[89] See Herris, *Germany's Fighter Competitions of 1918*, pp.66–67. Richthofen's successor as *JG* I's commander, *Hptm.* Wilhelm Reinhard, was killed during the adjunct trials while testing a Zeppelin-Dornier D.I on 3 July and Willy Gabriel said that Udet had been the favorite among *JG* I pilots to succeed him. Udet was a reserve officer, however, and it had been decreed that only a regular officer could lead a *Geschwader*. (see *Cross & Cockade* 3:4, p.344) The post went instead to Hermann Göring on 8 July. One can only wonder what the personal dynamics between Udet and Göring – and indeed their entire futures as well as Germany's – might have been like had Udet been assigned that role.

[90] For a detailed account of the fight, see *Over the Front* 19:2, pp.100–17.

[91] A flight from *Jasta* 17 later joined the melee and forced down another 27th Aero pilot, 1Lt. Clifford A. McElvain.

[92] *Cross & Cockade* 2:2, p.98.

[93] My thanks to Jean Devaux, Alan Toelle, and Greg VanWyngarden for providing the database.

[94] Karl Bodenschatz (*Jagd in Flanderns Himmel*, p.193) reported that when *JG* I moved to Monthussart-Ferme (i.e., Ferme du Mont Hussard), its pilots were quartered at "Braisne" and "Courcelles." The farm is located between Braine (not Braisne) and Courcelles-sur-Vesle.

[95] It has sometimes been asserted that their "rivalry" was not so friendly, but this is belied by Udet's numerous references to Loewenhardt as his "good friend" or "best buddy" in postwar interviews as well as the Loewenhardt portrait that was featured prominently on the wall of Udet's Berlin apartment.

[96] A biography of Udet's 51st victim can be found in Peter Kilduff's "From the Pulpit to the Cockpit – Lt. Charles L. Wood, Jr., RAF" (*Over the Front* 28:2). Wood was taken from the wreckage of his Sopwith Camel to a German field hospital, where he died a week later on 17 August 1918.

[97] pp.943–44. My thanks to Greg VanWyngarden for providing a copy of the article and to Adam Wait for his translation of it into English.

[98] Ishoven, *The Fall of an Eagle: The Life of Fighter Ace Ernst Udet*, p.146 states that LeRoy Prinz of the 27th Aero Squadron was the man Udet brought down for his 57th victory. Prinz, a colorful character and show-business professional, made that claim during a dinner held for Udet at the Biltmore Hotel (Los Angeles) in 1933, but there is no independent evidence to support his assertion.

[99] *Mein Fliegerleben*, pp.111–13.

[100] See Kilduff, *The Red Baron Combat Wing*, p.234.

[101] *Mein Fliegerleben*, pp.115–16.

[102] Ibid., photo between pp.104 and 105.

[103] Ibid., p.116.

[104] Udet had become personal friends with the company's founders, Gustav Otto and the Everbusch brothers (Alfred, Ernst, and Walter) during the war.

[105] Literally translated as "Neck and Leg break," it is equivalent to "Break a leg!"

[106] The framed piece of fabric is now on display at the National Museum of the United States Air Force in Dayton, Ohio.

[107] Ishoven, *The Fall of an Eagle: The Life of Fighter Ace Ernst Udet*, p.137.

[108] Ibid., p.142.

[109] Mahncke, *For Kaiser and Hitler*, p.115.

[110] Monkhouse, *Mercedes-Benz: Grand Prix Racing 1934–1955*, p.99. My thanks to Aaron Weaver for bringing this passage to my attention.

Left & Above: Udet drew these self-deprecating caricatures illustrating his status before and after acquiring fame. The first caption translates as "Without a Shoot-Down" and the second as "With 62 Shoot-Downs."

Facing Page: A portrait of Udet that was seen hanging in his study in the 1935 movie *Wunder des Fliegens*. It was based on a photo that was published in the 5 February 1929 edition of *La Vie Aérienne* and that originated during the same sitting as the one seen on page 50 above.

Ernst Udet – The Aircraft

Otto *Doppeldecker* and/or LVG B-type?
(February–late April 1915)

Udet began his flight training as a civilian pilot at Munich's Gustav Otto Flugmaschinenfabrik (Gustav Otto Flying Machine Factory) in February 1915. He earned his civilian pilot's license toward the end of April. We do not know what aircraft he trained in. The firm had its Otto *Doppeldecker* and was also producing LVG aircraft under license in 1915.

LVG B.I, B.II, Albatros B-type
(July–August 1915)

Udet received his military pilot's training with *FEA*

9 at Darmstadt from July through August 1915 with Hermann Weller as his instructor. Initially confined to ground personnel duties in late June, a frustrated Udet produced his civilian pilot's license at the Darmstadt school one day and: "I was allowed to fly an old LVG that same evening…"[1] This would have been either a B.I (introduced prewar) or a B.II (first in the field in December 1914). U1 is a portrait of Udet posing next to what appears to have been a modified LVG B.II. It has been identified as such because of its semicircular upper wing cutout, the deep line of its upper engine panel, and the widely-splayed landing gear struts; however, it has a rectangular access panel

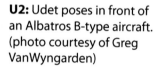

U1

U1: Udet poses in flight gear with what appears to have been a modified LVG B.II. (photo courtesy of Greg VanWyngarden)

U2: Udet poses in front of an Albatros B-type aircraft. (photo courtesy of Greg VanWyngarden)

U3–5: U3 shows Aviatik B.II 1327/15 almost over on its back before efforts were made (U4-U5) to right it on its wheels again. U5 was labeled "Udet's Crack-up" and seems to show a crew member in the pilot's rear cockpit in an apparent attempt to add weight to the tail to help bring it down. This may well have been the airplane that Udet and *Lt.* Bruno Justinus used on 14 September 1915 when they had to glide over Switzerland to reach German territory. (photo courtesy Bruno Schmäling)

rather than the usual circular panel seen on a B.II's nose. In addition, instead of the upper engine panel running down to the propeller opening like other LVG B.IIs, it seems to have had the style of nose cap seen on Albatros B.I and B.III types. Aircraft were often modified in the field, so these differences do not necessarily overrule its identity as an LVG B.II. U2 has Udet in front of an Albatros B-type airplane with no insignia on his collar – which means he was still a *Flieger* (private). He was promoted to *Gefreiter* not long after joining *AFA* 206 in September, so he probably was at the *Fliegerschule* (Aviation School) when U2 was taken. The *Fliegerschule* at Darmstadt possessed a wide variety of aircraft types, so Udet could easily have flown an Albatros B-type while there.

Aviatik Type 15 B.185/14, B.II 1327/15 (September 1915)

Udet joined *AFA* 206 on 4 September 1915 and served there less than a month before he was posted away to *AFP* Gaede on 2 October. While describing his flight with *Lt.* Bruno Justinus to bomb Belfort on 14 September, Udet wrote: "Our white Aviatik with the 120 Mercedes wafts along like a swan."[2] Aviatik B.IIs 1320–1355/15 were fitted with 120-hp Mercedes D.II engines, so their aircraft would have had a serial number in that range.[3] A little under two weeks

U2

U3

U4

U5

later, the pair crashed after their overloaded machine sideslipped onto their own airfield. Udet related that he was knocked unconscious and wrenched his knee badly whereas Justinus, who had jumped from the airplane just before impact, suffered multiple contusions and abrasions; both had to spend some time in the hospital. U3–5 come from an *AFA* 206 album that labeled U5 as *Bruch Udet* ("Udet's Crack-up"); and it depicts Aviatik B.II 1327/15, which indicates that this may well have been the aircraft Udet and Justinus were using on the 14th. We might have assumed that this was the aircraft

they later crashed in, too, except that U6, from the same *AFA* 206 collection, was also labeled "Udet's crack-up" and shows the wreckage of Aviatik Type 15 B.185/14. The aircraft in U3–5 seems to have nosed over without causing much damage to either men or machine (note what appears to be one of the crew members at left in U3), but the nature of U6's wreck could have been due to a sideslip to the ground and appears more likely to have caused the kinds of injuries that Udet described. In any event, we have clearly identified two aircraft that Udet flew during his brief tenure with *AFA* 206.

U6: This image was also labeled "Udet's Crack-up" in the same *AFA* 206 album. It captured Aviatik Type 15 B.185/14 in seriously damaged condition. It seems likely that this was the aircraft in which Udet and Justinus crashed onto their own airfield in late September 1915 – the crash that saw Udet serving time in a stockade as punishment. (photo courtesy of Bruno Schmäling)

U7: This image was published in *Mein Fliegerleben* (opposite p.25) with this caption (translated): "After the unsuccessful struggle with bedbugs in Neubreisach's military jail." This means the picture originated sometime after his release from the stockade but before he went to *KEK* Habsheim, and that Udet is leaning on an Otto-built LVG B.I that was at *AFP* Gaede. We do not know if he ever flew it though.

Fokker Eindeckers (including E.I 54/15, E.II 33/15, E.III 105/15, E.III 404/15)

(Late November 1915–September 1916)

Udet was assigned to *KEK* Habsheim in late November 1915, but before going there, he had to familiarize himself with rotary-engine aircraft. He did this at *AFP* Gaede (we do not know what he trained in) for a few days and then: "My machine, a brand new Fokker, arrives two days later. It looks wonderfully graceful, as sleek as a hawk. The old Aviatik B-machine that I flew at 206 looks as plump as a goose next to it."[4] It most likely was an E.III. He took off in it the same day but the machine unfortunately was wrecked when one of its cables got tangled and it crashed into a hangar (see U8). "The *Park* provided me with another machine, but this time it was an old Fokker. The next morning, I flew off to Habsheim."[5] This one may have been an E.II or even an E.I.

The Werksnummer (factory number) 305 visible on the right elevator of U9's Eindecker tells us that it is E.I 54/15. Udet is standing in the cockpit with KEK Habsheim pilots on the right side of the airplane and the unit's mechanics and other personnel on the left. It has been said that this image commemorated Udet's first victory on 18 March 1916. If not, it was certainly before then because he is not wearing the Iron Cross, 1st Class that he was given on 20 March as a result of that victory. U10 was taken the same time as U9 (in particular, note the propeller's identical position) and confirms that it was 54/15. Both U9 and U10 display colored sashes on either side of the white background that contain the fuselage's *cross pattée* insignia. The precise color of those sashes has been discussed by air historians for many years with multiple theories being offered. An examination of the history of 54/15 and *KEK* Habsheim might point to a new solution, however.

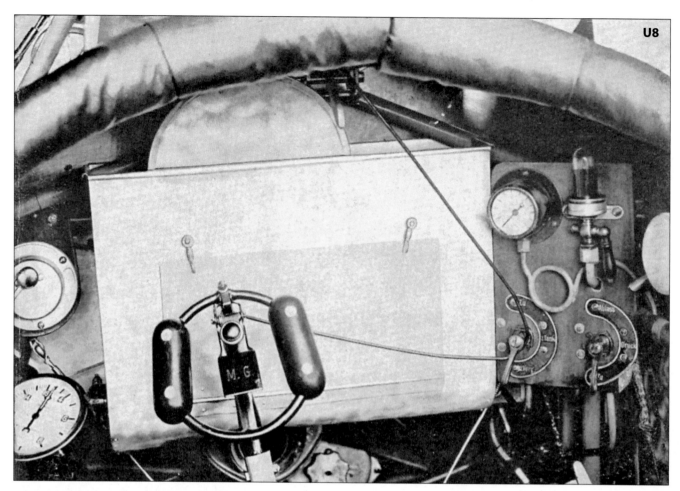

U8: The cockpit of the "brand new Fokker" *Eindecker* that Udet smashed into a hangar in late November 1915. An investigation later that evening determined that the machine gun cable on the control stick had been entangled by a fuel switch. This photo was provided as evidence.

U9-10: These images reportedly originated upon the occasion of Udet's first victory on 18 March 1916. The first shows Udet standing atop E.I 54/15 and surrounded by a variety of *KEK* Habsheim personnel. The second captures Udet posing in the cockpit. (second photo courtesy of the Richard Alexander [thanks section]1914–1918 Aviation Heritage Trust)

First, we know that *KEK* Habsheim was a detachment of either *FFA* 48 or *FFA* 68 and that it shared its airfield with those units.[6] *FFA*s 48 and 68 were both part of *Armee-Abteilung* Gaede that was known to have employed aircraft marked with diagonal black and white bands around the fuselage. U15 captures 54/15 around the time of its delivery to Habsheim (note the lack of fabric staining) and we can see that it bore one version of *AA* Gaede's black-and-white sash marking. U16 shows 54/15 after the white sash had been expanded to include the *cross pattée* insignia – another *AA* Gaede version. U32 (page 96) included a *KEK* Habsheim E.III in its background, but that aircraft carried only the standard *cross pattée* insignia on its fuselage. In that photo, Udet is not wearing the Iron Cross, 1st Class that he was awarded on 20 March as a result of his first victory two days earlier; so we know it

was taken before that event. U35 (page 97) appears to include the same aircraft seen in U32 and again, it bears only the standard fuselage insignia. In this instance, Udet is wearing his Iron Cross, 1st Class so we know this image originated after its award. U17 is a picture of *KEK* Habsheim's *Feldwebel* Herwarth Wendel and *Offz-Stv.* Willy Glinkermann in front of one of the unit's Fokker E.IVs which again has no special marking. This sequential evidence could indicate that *KEK* Habsheim dispensed with the *AA* Gaede sash markings sometime before 20 March 1916. U32 and U35 bracket Udet's 20 March Iron Cross award; so if U9 and U10 indeed commemorate his first victory or at least originated not very long before it, then they too occurred sometime after the *AA Gaede* markings had been abandoned. Accordingly, the 54/15 colored sashes seen in them may simply have been an effort to eradicate the

U9

former *AA* Gaede marking, which is clearly evident underneath; and the overpainted sash color may have been an attempt to match the usual fuselage color – that is, beige. It would have appeared slightly lighter because it had not yet been weathered and stained like the rest of the fuselage. Having said all this, the beige concept remains a theory based on available evidence and is by no means proven.

On a final note, the Egyptian hieroglyphs visible on the aft portion of Udet's 54/15 in U10 were *djed* (stability in life/hope in the afterlife), *ankh* (eternal life) and the *was* scepter (power). They were Egypt's three most important symbols and were used everywhere in Egyptian art, writing, sarcophagi, etc. – and often together. Why Udet had them on his airplane is a mystery, however.

U10

U11

U11–14: Four more pictures of E.I 54/15. In the first, an unknown NCO pilot exits its cockpit and its serial number can be seen between his feet. In the second, Udet is now in its cockpit. For some reason, the serial number does not show up in this print but all other aspects of the airplane (e.g., fuselage stains, folds in cockpit side combing) match. The third features Udet again in a closeup shot. He is not wearing the Iron Cross, 1st Class he was awarded on 20 March 1916, so this photo occurred before then. The fourth offers a full portside view. (photos courtesy of the 1914–1918 Aviation Heritage Trust)

U12

U13

U18–U20 are three images of Udet with a nosed-over Fokker E.II 33/15 that were assigned a date of 6 December 1915 in one of Udet's albums. Curiously, we know that E.II 33/15 was flown by *Uffz.* Eduard Böhme of *FFA* 9b, which was stationed at the time near Udet's *KEK* Habsheim at Colmar North airfield.

U15: E.I 54/15 at Habsheim airfield. The black and white sashes on its fuselage were one of *Armee-Abteilung* Gaede's markings for aircraft serving under it. The lack of staining and weathering on the aircraft indicates that it was fairly new when the photograph was taken. (photo courtesy of Greg VanWyngarden)

The aircraft here still bears *FFA* 9b's markings and a comparison of the stains on the starboard fuselage just aft of the wing with those when Böhme flew it (U21) confirms that it indeed was 33/15. The treeline in the photos suggests that the site was Colmar North airfield, so what was Udet doing flying it there on 6 December 1915?

U22 shows Udet standing in front of Fokker E.III 105/15 soon after it had overturned, and judging by his flight gear and smile of relief, he had been the one piloting it. Note that the E.III had been decorated in *Armee-Abteilung* Gaede's black-and-white sash marking as well as a black rudder. U23 shows someone in the cockpit of Fokker E.III 105/15 that

U16: Another picture of E.I 54/15 at Habsheim airfield. At this point, it is bearing another version of *AA* Gaede's sash marking, where the white sash was expanded to accommodate *cross pattée* insignias. Udet is the man marked with an 'x'.

several sources have claimed was Udet. Independent support is offered by U1 above and U22, where Udet appears to be wearing the same flight coat and gloves and has the same type of German flight helmet seen in U23. U24, found in one of Udet's personal albums, displays 105/15 as its machine gun was being sighted

U17: *Feldwebel* Herwarth Wendel (left) and *Offz-Stv*. Willy Glinkermann (right) stand in front of a Fokker E.IV. There is a Fokker D.II or D.III behind it, indicating that the image was taken after *KEK* Habsheim had been folded into *Jasta* 15. Nevertheless, we know the E.IV would have been delivered to the unit months earlier when it was still *KEK* Habsheim. We have no record of Udet having flown a Fokker E.IV. (photo courtesy of Greg VanWyngarden)

U18

U18–20: Three photos of Udet with Fokker E.II 33/15 that he evidently crashed on 6 December 1915. We know that prior to this, the machine had been used by *FFA* 9b at Colmar North airfield, and it indeed still bears the fuselage marking of that unit. (photos courtesy of the 1914-1918 Aviation Heritage Trust)

U19

U20

U20-blowup

U21

U21: *Uffz*. Eduard Böhme sits atop Fokker E.II 33/15. The enlarged section shows the same fuselage stains evident in U20 above. The only thing missing is the "E…3/15" which appears to have worn off by the time Udet flew it.

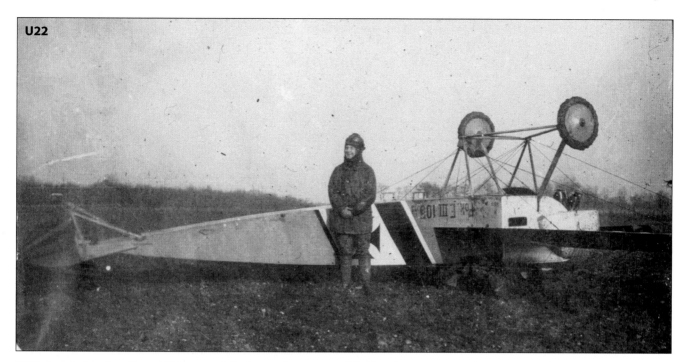

U22: An obviously relieved Udet stands in front of overturned Fokker E.III 105/15. At this point, the fighter was still decorated with *Armee-Abteilung* Gaede's black-and-white sash marking. (photo courtesy of the 1914–1918 Aviation Heritage Trust)

U23: Someone often identified as Udet sits in the cockpit of E.III 105/15. It bears the same distinctive fuselage sash design seen on Udet's E.I 54/15 in U9–14 above.

U24

U24: Here we see a mechanic sighting in the machine gun mounted on E.III 105/15. The photo comes from one of Udet's personal albums.

U25–26. Two pictures of Udet in E.III 105/15. Note the P08 Luger pistol with shoulder stock that is affixed to the cockpit's starboard side. Exactly what role it was meant to fill when the aircraft had a machine gun is difficult to know. (photos courtesy of Joachim Serger Collection via Josef Scott)

in and leaves little doubt that Udet flew this airplane. The overpainted sash design on the fuselage in U23 and U24 is identical to that seen on Udet's E.I 54/15; but again, this may not have been a personal marking and might only have been an attempt to cover over an abandoned *AA* Gaede design. U25 and U26 are two photos of Udet in the same aircraft. We know this because U24 has the same shoulder-stocked Luger P08 pistol arrangement attached to its cockpit's starboard side. U27 captures E.III 105/15 being re-armed under the watchful eye of Udet who is examining the machine gun's ammunition feed belt. Finally, U28–U30 display the aircraft's port side while U31 catches it taking off.

U32 is a photo of Udet in front of Fokker E.III 40?/15 (the third number is obscured in this image), but we can identify it as 404/15 because of U33, which shows the same aircraft with Udet standing in front of it at *KEK* Habsheim. Note the anemometer device on the leading edge of the port wing in both images, which as far as we know was not a common field modification. U33 shows that it underwent some changes after U32 was snapped: (i) repainted

serial number, (ii) repainted or new rudder displaying smaller national insignia, and (iii) a small, light-colored band on the aft portion of the fuselage. U34 appears to capture the same aircraft after the light fuselage band had been added; however, the national insignia on the fuselage looks to have been crudely repainted and the rudder insignia is of the standard size. In U32, Udet is not wearing the Iron Cross 1st Class he was awarded on 20 March 1916 and his rank insignia are that of an *Unteroffizier*, which he became on 28 November 1915, so it was taken sometime in between. His Iron Cross is present in U35, so it originated after 20 March but before he was transferred to *Jasta* 15 in October 1916.

Pfalz E.I
(Late November 1915—April? 1916)
U33 and U34 (see below) contain Pfalz E.I *Eindeckers* that are present alongside known *KEK* Habsheim aircraft. Although we have no direct evidence that Udet flew one or more of them, it seems reasonable to assume that he did on at least a few occasions.

U25

U26

U27: Udet inspects E.III 105/15's ammunition belt as his mechanics service and load its machine gun. (photo courtesy of the 1914–1918 Aviation Heritage Trust)

U28–30: Three images of E.III 105/15 on the ground. Udet is posing before it in the first and is the man petting the dog while *Uffz*. Karl Weingärtner watches in the second. (photos courtesy of the 1914–1918 Aviation Heritage Trust)

U29

U30

Pfalz E.IV 647/15
(April--? 1916)

U37 is a photo of Udet in the cockpit of Pfalz E.IV 647/15 (the serial number is just visible on the fuselage beneath him). He is wearing the Iron Cross, 1st Class that he was awarded on 20 March 1916 and he conveniently autographed the photo in May

1916. Five of the first batch of six E.IVs (numbered 642–648/15) were in the field as of 30 April 1916, so it is fairly certain that *KEK* Habsheim had 647/15 by then.[7] U38 is an image of presumably the same aircraft. Some publications have mistakenly identified it as having been damaged by Udet; however, Udet's personal album called it "*Bruch*

U31

U31: Fokker E.III 105/15 lifts off from its airfield. (photo courtesy of the 1914–1918 Aviation Heritage Trust)

U32

U32: *Uffz.* Ernst Udet (center) is flanked by *Uffz.* Karl Weingärtner (left) and *Lt.* Otto Pfältzer. Behind them is *KEK* Habsheim's Fokker E.III 40?/15 (probably 404/15). Udet is not wearing the Iron Cross, 1st Class he won on 20 March 1916, so the photo originated sometime before that.

U33: Ernst Udet poses in front of two of *KEK* Habsheim's *Eindecker* fighters: E.III 404/15 (foreground) and E.III 105/15 (background). A Pfalz E.I is at far right and the cowling of another Pfalz *Eindecker* is just visible behind it. (photos courtesy of the 1914–1918 Aviation Heritage Trust)

U33

U34

U35

U34: E.III 404/15, with a light-colored band around its aft fuselage, rests near some tents and a Pfalz E.I fighter. The man in the foreground appears to be *Lt.* Otto Pfältzer. (photo courtesy of the 1914–1918 Aviation Heritage Trust)

U35: The original contingent of *KEK* Habsheim pilots after Udet joined them. Left to right: *Lt.* Otto Pfältzer, *Uffz.* Karl Weingärtner, *Vzfw.* Ernst Udet, *Gefr.* Willy Glinkermann. They are posing in front of a Fokker E.III that displays the same anemometer device on its port wing that is seen in U32 and U33. Udet is now displaying his Iron Cross, 1st Class (and Pfältzer has grown a moustache) so the image was created after 20 March 1916.

U38

U36: *Uffz.* Karl Weingärtner (far left), Udet (second from left), and three other men pose in front of what presumably was E.III 404/15. Just visible under its port wing in the background is E.III 105/15. (photo courtesy of the 1914–1918 Aviation Heritage Trust)

U37: Udet poses in the cockpit of Pfalz E.IV 647/15. He is wearing the same French crash helmet that he apparently took from one of the crewmen of his first victory. (photo courtesy of Greg VanWyngarden)

U38: This Pfalz E.IV has been identified in other works as one that Udet damaged while at *KEK* Habsheim; however, Udet's personal album said it had been damaged by *Lt.* Willy Glinkermann in June 1916. Given the rarity of E.IVs at the front, it is probably 647/15 as seen in U37 at left. (photo courtesy of Greg VanWyngarden)

U39: Udet poses in the cockpit of a Fokker D.II fighter.

U39

U40

U40-41: Udet stands next to D.III 368/16. He had a metal facsimile of an observer's head and shoulders attached to its upper fuselage "in order to deceive the enemy" – that is, to fool them into thinking he was flying a two-seater.

U41

Glinkermann, Juni 1916" ("Glinkermann's crash, June 1916") We do not know when Udet stopped flying a Pfalz E.IV.

Fokker D.II, Fokker D.III 368/16, D.III 1017/16?
(October 1916–January 1917)
When *Jasta* 15 became operational on 9 October 1916, it was stocked with Fokker D.II and D.III

U42: An overturned Fokker D.III 1017/16 that Peter Grosz attributed to Udet. (photo courtesy of Greg VanWyngarden)

aircraft. U39 is a picture of Udet in the cockpit of a Fokker D.II (note the single machine gun). U40–41 capture Udet standing with D.III 368/16, which he had fitted with a a sheet metal facsimile of an observer's head and shoulders *"um den Feind zu täuschen"* ("in order to deceive the enemy").[8] U41 depicts Udet wearing the ribbon for Württemberg's Merit Cross with Swords that he received on 4 November 1916, so we know it originated sometime afterward. U40, apparently taken at the same time (note the diagonal shadow under the cockpit and falling across the fuselage insignia), also includes

U43: Udet stands in front of Albatros D.III 1941/16 while his mechanics, Walter Behrend and Gunkelmann, service the engine. Alex Imrie, in his *German Fighter Units 1914–May 1917*, provided this detailed account, which we assume came from his contact with Walter Behrend: "Lt. Ernst Udet of *Jagdstaffel* 15 waits by his Albatros D III (1941/16) while mechanics Gunkelmann and Behrend work on the cooling system at Habsheim aerodrome, 1 January 1917 [but see endnote 10]. Despite draining the system, at very low temperatures ice formed around the vanes of the circulator pump, which necessitated flushing with hot water before replenishing the coolant for flight. The air temperature when this photograph was taken was -20 degrees Centigrade."

U44: Udet sits in the cockpit of an early Albatros D.V. (photo courtesy of 1914–1918 Aviation Heritage Trust)

an Albatros D.II in the background (left) as well as another Fokker D.III (right).

Albatros D.III 1941/16
(Late January–May/June 1917)

Udet stated in *Kreuz wider Kokarde* (p.53) that he and *Lt.* Willy Glinkermann were flying "two brand-new Albatros D.III aircraft" when he brought down a Nieuport that we are fairly certain was his fourth victory on 20 February 1917. U43 shows Udet and his two mechanics working on Albatros D.III 1941/16, which was probably delivered to the front in late January 1917.[10] This may have been the new D.III to which he was referring. Udet almost certainly flew one or more D.IIIs until the D.V was introduced in May/June 1917.

Albatros D.V
(May/June–4 August 1917)

U44 has Udet in the cockpit of an early Albatros D.V.

We know this because of the wooden headrest that was supplied with the first D.Vs that appeared at the front in May/June 1917. Most pilots were critical of the headrest, however, and had it removed to allow for better viewing behind them – and the Albatros firm eventually dispensed with it altogether. Albatros expert Charles Gosse has provided several more reasons why this D.V was probably from that type's first batch (1000/17–1199/17): (i) it does not display the paper rigging placard between the cabane struts that began to be used from around 1192/17 on, (ii) it possesses padding around the headrest that was dispensed with as early as 1021/17, (iii) the trim around the windscreen and padding in front of it have not disappeared as they did after use on other D.Vs, and (iv) the striped seatbelt was used on early D.Vs. So it appears that Udet had this image taken while with *Jasta* 15. He did not achieve any victories in whatever he was flying during this period with *Jasta* 15 and moved on to *Jasta* 37 on 6 August 1917.

U45–46: Udet's silver-colored Albatros D.V at *Jasta* 37. It may have been the first aircraft to which he attached "LO," the nickname for his girlfriend. (photos courtesy of Greg VanWyngarden)

U47: Udet's silver-colored Albatros D.V in flight. Note the flight leader's streamers attached to the tail.

U45

U46

U47

U48

U49

U50

U48: Udet (left) and *Lt.* Heinrich Schleth stand arm-in-arm in front of the same airplane. Schleth left *Jasta* 37 for *Jasta* 29 on 7 November 1917. (photo courtesy of Greg VanWyngarden)

U49: Someone strongly resembling Udet holds a conversation next to *Jasta* 37's Albatros D.III 2131/16 at Metz airfield. *Jasta* 37 was stationed there from 10 March through 18 July 1917 – before Udet joined the unit on 6 August. It appears that Udet was merely visiting *Jasta* 37 before joining it and that he did not actually fly D.III 2131/16, which was captured in this photo by happenstance. (photo courtesy of Greg VanWyngarden)

U50, U50-blowup: This lineup of *Jasta* 37 aircraft at Metz airfield demonstrates that D.III 2131/16 (second from the left) belonged to the unit prior to Udet's arrival. (photo courtesy of Greg VanWyngarden)

U50 blowup

U51: A side view of Albatros D.V 4476/17 while maintenance was being performed on its engine. (photo courtesy of Greg VanWyngarden)

U51

U51a: A side view of Albatros D.V 4476/17 showing a bullet hole that has been patched and marked with British cockades. (photo courtesy of Greg VanWyngarden)

U52: A closer view of Albatros D.V 4476/17 with Udet in the cockpit. Note the bullet holes that have been patched and marked with British cockades – one just under the cockpit coaming and another to the left of the 'L' in "LO." (photo courtesy of Greg VanWyngarden)

Albatros D.V

(6 August–September? 1917)

Udet's combat report for 17 September 1917 stated that he was in D.V 4476/17, which had probably arrived only a short time before (see below). So what was he flying before then upon his arrival at *Jasta* 37? The answer is that we do not know; but U45–47 offer one possibility. The D.V in those photographs was painted mostly silver but also carried *Jasta* 37's unit marking of a black-and-white, diagonally-striped tailplane and wheel covers with black bars on them. As we shall see, available evidence indicates that Udet flew D.V 4476/17 up through his appointment as *Jasta* 37's CO and beyond, and then switched over to a black-fuselaged D.Va. Where his silver-colored D.V might have figured into this mix is difficult to determine, but the period 6 August up through the delivery of 4476/17 in September offers a tempting time slot; and U48 provides circumstantial support for this theory. In it, Udet is standing next to

Lt. Heinrich Schleth, who departed *Jasta* 37 for *Jasta* 29 on 7 November 1917. We know that Udet flew 4476/17 from September to Schleth's departure date, so unless Udet alternated between 4476/17 and his silver mount, he would have flown it beforehand. If so, then it appears that it was the first of his aircraft to employ "LO" on its fuselage – the nickname for his girlfriend, Eleonore Zink.

We should mention one other photo here. U49 is a picture of someone closely resembling Udet (with his back to the camera) holding some type of discussion next to *Jasta* 37's Albatros D.III 2131/16 at Metz-Frescaty airdrome (note the large Zeppelin hangar in the background). U50 shows the same aircraft in a *Jasta* 37 lineup at Metz airfield, which the unit occupied from 10 March through 18 July 1917. Although some understandably have suggested that Udet flew this machine at *Jasta* 37, it should be pointed out that he did not join the unit until 6 August (he was transferred the day before), at which

U53: This image appeared in *Mein Fliegerleben* (opposite p.57) and was captioned "*So sieht ein Jagdflieger aus, der vor 15 Minuten 'Saures' bezog. Behrend zählte 21 Treffer in der treuen Albatros D V!*" ("This is how a combat pilot looks who had been given hell 15 minutes earlier. Behrend [Udet's mechanic] counted 21 hits in the trusty Albatros D.V!") More bullet holes appear in this highly-edited photo than the two that had been patched in U52, so someone took the liberty of adding them in.

U54: Udet, standing in front of his hangared Albatros D.V 4476/17, labeled this photo "CO of *Jagdstaffel 37*."

U55-56: Albatros D.V 4476/17 (note the bullet hole patch to the left of the 'L' in "LO" also evident in U52) appears in a lineup of *Jasta* 37's black Albatros fighters. Udet ordered this change in marking after he was made the unit's CO on 7 November 1917. (first photo courtesy of Greg VanWyngarden; second photo courtesy of Bruno Schmäling)

U57-58: These photos show the underside of an Albatros fighter marked with a light-colored "U." for Udet. This may be the fighter he described as an "Albatros, yellow fuselage, striped tailplane with two streamers" on 9 March 1918 or it might have been D.Va 5368/17 (see below) instead. (first photo courtesy of the 1914–1918 Aviation Heritage Trust)

point *Jasta* 37 was at Phalempin airfield. It appears then that Udet was merely visiting *Jasta* 37 at Metz when U49 was snapped – perhaps to check on the status of his 4 June application to join it. It is therefore unlikely that he actually flew D.III 2131/16, which just happened to be caught in the photograph.

Albatros D.V 4476/17

(September–November 1917? or March 1918?)
As mentioned earlier, Udet's 17 September 1917 combat report, translated and published in a 1931 edition of the *Toronto Star*, specified that he was flying Albatros D.V 4476/17. This D.V was from the third batch that had been ordered and was technically the 674th to have been assigned its

U57

U58

U59 & U59 Blowup: *Jasta* 37's black Albatros number '3' takes off in front of an Albatros with a black spinner and light-colored fuselage. The enlarged section shows signs of a 'U' under its lower port wing as seen in U57–58 above. The aircraft lineup is the same as seen in U55, so this leaves little doubt that the light-bodied Albatros was Udet's 4476/17. (photo courtesy of Bruno Schmäling)

U60–64: Five views of Udet's black Albatros D.Va at *Jasta* 37. The fourth (and its enlarged section) and fifth ones show the aircraft taking off. (first photo courtesy of Greg VanWyngarden; second, third, and fifth images courtesy of Bruno Schmäling; fourth photo courtesy of 1914–1918 Aviation Heritage Trust)

military serial number. German records state that 640 of the type were at the front as of 31 August 1917, so it would appear that 4476/17 would have been delivered around the end of August/early September.[11] U51–54 are four pictures of that aircraft. U54 was captioned *"Führer der Jagdstaffel 37"* ("CO of *Jagdstaffel* 37") in *Mein Fliegerleben* (opposite p.64) and U55 and U56 have 4476/17 in

a lineup of black *Jasta* 37 aircraft – both of which indicate that he flew it at least up until he was the *Staffelführer* (on 7 November) and subsequently mandated that the *Staffel*'s aircraft have black fuselages. The dilemma this presents, however, concerns the Albatros he was flying on 18 October 1917 following his 14th victory that day. He said that after it was shot up by a flight of Sopwiths, he

U60

U61

U62

U63

U63 blowup

U65: Udet's black Albatros D.Va is at far right at the end of this *Jasta* 37 lineup. (photo courtesy of Greg VanWyngarden)

U66: The result of Udet's emergency landing in his black Albatros D.Va.

U67: Udet identified this photo as having been taken right after his fight with 2Lt. Charles R. Maasdorp on 28 March 1918. The tension and exhaustion he experienced are clearly evident on his face.

was forced to land close to the lines, rolled it into a flooded ditch, and then British artillery opened up on it. If it was 4476/17, then it must have been recovered and repaired since it appears in U55–56. If that aircraft was destroyed or unsalvageable, however, then it could not have been 4476/17; so what was it?

On the other hand, he have a handwritten note from Udet to a balloon company that was sold in an auction several years ago that asked if they could attest to the downing of an airplane on 9 March 1918. A translation of its opening sentence reads: "Around 10:40 a.m. today, I (Albatros, yellow fuselage, striped tailplane with two streamers) had a serious, lengthy dogfight with a Sopwith which then went down just behind the English lines."[12] Of particular note is the fact that he pointedly

was not flying an Albatros with a black fuselage at the time. We have U57, which came from Udet's personal album, and U58 which show the underside of an Albatros D.V/Va with a light-colored "U." on its lower wing, a black spinner, and a light-colored fuselage. Furthermore, we have U59, an image that was shot the same time as U55 and U56. The enlarged section shows signs of a "U" on an Albatros fighter's lower wing exactly as seen in U57–58, and in all three pictures it looks identical to 4476/17 in U51–54. So is this the Albatros he described during his search for witnesses of his 9 March 1918 victory? If so, then we would have certain evidence that he kept 4476/17 as a spare right up into March 1918. It is also possible, however, that the Albatros he used for his 9 March 1918 had been D.Va 5368/17 (see below).

U68: This Dr.I appears in the background of the picture of a *Jasta* 11 triplane's crash on 2 May 1918. It displays chevron markings that Udet is known to have employed on other of his aircraft. Was this Dr.I 149/17? (photo courtesy of Greg VanWyngarden)

Albatros D.Va
(November 1917 – ?)

U60–66 show Udet's Albatros D.Va that had its fuselage painted black to conform with the *Staffel* markings he had established after taking command of *Jasta* 37 on 7 November 1917. Instead of large numbers on either side of its nose, however (as seen on the rest of the unit's aircraft in U55–U56), he substituted large chevrons to denote his leadership position. The first D.Vas came to the front in October 1917 so it is plausible that he might have first flown his in November. U55–56 above strongly suggest that while he was having it painted black, he continued to use D.V 4476/17. Udet related in *Kreuz wider Kokarde* (pp.109–12) that following a fight during which his black D.Va's fuel tanks were pierced, he had to make an emergency landing at his airfield: "So I set down with a tailwind and roared at high speed over the field into a low-lying lane. The undercarriage, which had been weakened by

a ricochet, collapsed, and the result was that my good, brave, black Albatros machine completely overturned. Subsequently, several hits were found in the engine, the fuselage, the wings, and tail." U66 captured the result, which Udet labeled as *"Das Ende meines treuen Einsitzers"* ("The end of my trusty single-seater.")[13] Unfortunately, he never said when this accident occurred, so we do not know when he had to switch to another aircraft.

Albatros D.Va 5368/17
(Late December 1917–March 1918?)

Udet's claim report for his 18th victory on 28 January 1918 mentioned that his aircraft had been "Albatros D.V. 5368/17" (see above, p.24). That serial number actually belonged to the 204th D.Va given a military designation; and since there were 239 of that type at the front as of 31 December 1917, it is likely that it arrived at *Jasta* 37 in the last half of that month. Udet also included a drawing of the tail of the aircraft that

U69–70: Udet's hand-me-down Dr.I 586/17 from Hans Kirschstein is at right in both of these photographs. The men in the first (left to right): *Lt.* Julius Bender, *Lt.* Egon Koepsch, *Lt.* Carlos Meyer-Baldó (back to camera), *Lt.* Heinrich Drekmann, *Lt.* Heinrich Maushake (on the ground near the wingtip), Udet. In the second (left to right): Bender, Maushake, Koepsch, Meyer-Baldó, Drekmann. (photos courtesy of Greg VanWyngarden)

depicted *Jasta* 37's marking of a diagonally-striped tailplane. He added his leader streamers trailing behind it but did not color in the rear fuselage. Was this merely an oversight or was it intentional – that is, its fuselage was not black? If it had been an oversight and the fuselage had been black, we could interpret this in several ways: (i) This was the black D.Va with chevrons that was later written off after an emergency landing. This would mean that he flew something else (D.V 4476/17 as seen in U51 above?) before receiving D.Va 5368/17 in late December and having it painted black. (ii) This was another black D.Va that Udet flew after his first one had been written off following an emergency landing. (iii) Udet alternated between his first black D.Va and this one after its arrival in late December until his first one was written off in an emergency landing. If the omission of black on the drawing's tail was intentional, however, this would be a strong indication that his black D.Va had already been written off and that he had switched to this aircraft. It would then be possible for it to have been the aircraft he used on 9 March 1918, described as having a "yellow fuselage, striped tailplane with two streamers."

Fokker Dr.I 149/17
(24 March–early April 1918)
U67 is a photo of Udet in a Fokker Dr.I that he said was snapped right after his fight with 2Lt. Charles R. Maasdorp on 28 March 1918.[14] During Udet's description of the fight for David Rogers that was published in the May 1931 edition of *Fawcett's Battle Stories*, he specified that he had been flying "Fokker Dr.I 149/17."[15] So this was the Dr.I Udet flew for the brief time he was with *Jasta* 11 before he went home on leave from early April through mid-May 1918. But what did the rest of it look like? Greg VanWyngarden and Jörn Leckscheid have offered an intriguing possibility. U68 comes from the background of a *Jasta* 11 photo capturing the aftermath of *Vzfw.* Edgar Scholtz's fatal crash on 2 May 1918. The Dr.I in U68 bears the chevron symbol that Udet employed on his black Albatros at *Jasta* 37 and the tailplane/elevator chevron that he later used on Fokker Dr.I 593/17 and at least two of his Fokker D.VIIs. What is missing is "LO!" on the fuselage. But Udet was home on leave when this image was taken and the aircraft was undoubtedly being used by another pilot; so what looks like a

U70

dark rectangular patch under the cockpit may have been where the "LO!" emblem was painted over or otherwise removed. Admittedly, this identification is purely speculative but there is a certain amount of logic to it.

Fokker Dr.I 586/17
(22 May–early June? 1918)

Shortly after Udet returned from leave, he was placed in charge of *Jasta* 4 on 22 May 1918. *Jastas* 6 and 11 received their first Fokker D.VIIs at this time and some of their Dr.Is were handed down to *Jasta* 4, including Hans Kirschtein's 586/17. Kirschstein had had diagonal black and white stripes applied to his aircraft's top wing (upper and under surfaces), rear fuselage, and interplane struts in the belief that this would throw off the enemy's aim during a dogfight. U69–U74, taken at *Jasta* 4's Cramoiselle airfield (just west of Cramaille) demonstrate that Udet retained those markings and had "LO!" added to the sides of its fuselage. According to Alex Imrie, the aircraft was subsequently put out of action "following an engine failure when, apparently, a detached cylinder removed the cowling in flight and tore the metal engine bulkhead" – an assessment based on U74's

image.[16] Unfortunately, we do not know when this accident occurred. We do know that Udet subsequently switched over to Dr.I 593/17 before receiving his first D.VII in late June 1918. So we can speculate that the accident occurred sometime around early June.

Fokker Dr.I 593/17
(June 1918)

We know from the shed in the background that U75 also originated at *Jasta* 4's airfield at Cramoiselle. Identified as Dr.I 593/17 by Alex Imrie (who knew and interviewed Udet's faithful mechanic, Walter Behrend, who accompanied Udet from one assignment to another), a small "LO!" emblem has been added to the fuselage just aft of the cockpit.[17] U76 provides a similar view with the addition of what appears to have been a light outline farther aft that was meant to serve as the base for a larger version. U77 is almost certainly the same aircraft (note what seems to be the small "LO!" emblem behind the cockpit), but here we can see that a chevron had been applied to its tailplane. Udet probably did not fly this Dr.I for very long because he switched to a D.VII by the end of June 1918.

U71

U71 Blowup

U72

U72 Blowup

U71: Another picture of Dr.I 586/17. The enlarged section of the image shows the tip of Udet's "LO!" insignia on the side of the fuselage. (photo courtesy of Greg VanWyngarden)

U72: Various airmen lounge in the shade provided by Udet's Dr.I 586/17. The "O" and an obscured "L" from Udet's "LO!" insignia are just visible in the enlargement of this grainy image. (photo courtesy of Greg VanWyngarden)

U73

U73 Blowup

U73: Dr.I 586/17 is at far left in this lineup of *Jasta* 4 triplanes. (photo courtesy of the 1914–1918 Aviation Heritage Trust)

U74: Dr.I 586/17 after its engine failed and put it out of action. (photo courtesy of Greg VanWyngarden)

U74

U75: Udet in another Dr.I following the loss of 586/17. Alex Imrie identified it as 593/17. (photo courtesy of Greg VanWyngarden)

U76: Another sideview of Udet's Dr.I 593/17. Just to the right of the "LO!" emblem is what appears to have been a light outline for a future, larger version of it. (photo courtesy of Greg VanWyngarden)

U77

U77: A view of Dr.I 593/17 from behind that shows the chevron that was present on its tailplane. (photo courtesy of Greg VanWyngarden)

The following sections on Udet's Fokker D.VII aircraft owe much to the research conducted by Greg VanWyngarden and German air historian Jörn Leckscheid.

Fokker D.VII (OAW) – two aircraft

(First machine 13–29 June 1918; second machine 13 June–August? 1918)

Jasta 4 received its first delivery of Fokker D.VIIs, license-built by the Ostdeutsche Albatros Werke (OAW) and powered by Mercedes D.IIIa engines, on 13 June 1918. U78 is an oft-published photo of one of them that Udet identified in *Mein Fliegerleben* (between pp.88 and 89) as "the airplane from which I had to make a parachute jump one day later." This was a reference to his escape on 29 June after which his D.VII crashed and was destroyed. U79–80 contain a similar-looking D.VII in the background with three important differences: (i) the upper wing, when examined closely under a computer program that lightens the hangar shadow, does not appear to have been striped, (ii) the chevron on the elevator extends all the way to its outer edge, and (iii) there is no inscription on the elevator.[18] Moreover, Jörn Leckscheid has presented convincing evidence that U79–U82 originated in late July and August

after Udet's "*Du doch nicht!!*" machine had been lost – so they depict a different D.VII (OAW). We must therefore conclude that it was a backup to his "*Du doch nicht!!*" mount – and perhaps the "new machine" Udet said he took up after his escape on 29 June before switching over to Fokker-built, BMW D.III-powered D.VIIF 378/18 on 1 July (see below). Evidently, he continued to use this second D.VII (OAW) aircraft as a spare after that.

Fokker D.VIIF 378/18

1–3? July 1918

In his postwar autobiography titled *Richthofen Flieger, Jasta* 6 pilot and ace *Lt.* Richard Wenzl disclosed: "On 22 June, the first B.M.W.-Fokkers (Fokker D.VII with 220-hp Bavarian engines) arrived and were placed in the hands of *Jasta* 11. The *Kanonen* [of the other *JG* I units] received one each as well."[19] Udet related that he was one of those *Kanonen* (literally 'big guns' but equivalent to 'aces') in his article, "My Experiences with the B.M.W. Motor Type IIIa": "I quickly obtained two of these new crates from the man then in command."[20] He also mentioned that he began testing it a few days before he lost his "*Du doch nicht!!*" D.VII (OAW) on 29 June. Udet elaborated further during

U78: A rear view of the Fokker D.VII (OAW) that Udet parachuted from and lost on 29 June 1918. The famous inscription on the elevator had a meaning equivalent to 'You and who else?' The upper wing, interplane struts, and even the gap between Udet's right arm and body were heavily 'touched up' in the negative that produced this image.

U79–80: According to convincing evidence presented by Jörn Leckscheid, these images show Udet at *Jasta* 4's Ferme du Mont Hussard airfield before the unit moved from that location to Ferme de Puisieux on 31 July/1 August. A D.VII (OAW) bearing his "LO!" insignia is in the background and is similar although not identical to the one appearing in U78. In the first picture, Udet is second from the left (on the telephone) and in the second, he is at far left (unbuttoning his tunic). (first photo courtesy of Jörn Leckscheid, second photo courtesy of Greg VanWyngarden)

his interview with David B. Rogers, published in *Fawcett's Battle Stories* as "How I Shot Down 62 Planes – From the War Log of Ernst Udet": "On July 1, 1918, accompanied by Lieut. Drekman [*sic*], in Fokker D-7 (378), I was loafing around at a height of 18,000 feet…"[21] Udet had recalled the serial number accurately because he had referred to his flight log.[22] The next day, Udet shot down 1Lt. Walter Wanamaker's Nieuport 28 and landed next to it to inspect the unfamiliar aircraft type as well as to inquire after its occupant. U83 purportedly captured that scene and, according to Fokker expert Jörn Leckscheid, indeed displays signs of a BMW-powered

D.VII from the first production batch: machine guns mounted in a high position and an Axial propeller with broad tips. In addition, the aircraft has early collector-style exhausts that exit through the side engine panels as well as hints of what was Udet's "LO!" insignia ahead of the fuselage cross. So it may well be an image of D.VIIF 378/18. U84 and U85 might show the same aircraft because (i) it too has high-mounted machine guns indicative of a BMW-powered machine, (ii) the placement of the "LO!" marking on its fuselage is identical to that seen in U83, and (iii) the "LO!" insignia style is different than D.VIIF 4253/18's (see below). In fact,

U79

U80

U81

Fliegerleutnant Ernſt Udet (×) im Kreiſe der Kameraden ſeiner Jagdſtaffel. Der junge Fliegerheld, der 60 feindliche Flugzeuge zum Abſturz brachte, verlobte ſich mit der Tochter des Kommerzienrats Alexander Zink in Roth.

U82

U82 Blowup

U81, 82, 82 Blowup: Two snapshots allegedly taken at *Jasta* 4's airfield outside of Bernes in mid-August 1918. Udet's spare D.VII (OAW) appears at right in both. In the first (from a newspaper), left to right: unknown, *Lt*. Hans-Georg von der Osten (reassigned to *Jasta* 11 on 10 August), *Lt*. Heinrich Maushake, Udet, *Lt*. Richard Kraut, *Lt*. Johannes Jessen, *Herr* Imhoff (BMW Company), *Lt*. Egon Koepsch. In the second, left to right: Kraut, Koepsch, Maushake, Jessen, unknown, Udet, Imhoff, unknown. (photos courtesy of Greg VanWyngarden)

U83: A very poor-quality image that allegedly shows Udet's Fokker D.VII after he had landed it next to 1Lt. Walter Wanamaker's downed Nieuport 28 on 2 July 1918. If so, it was D.VIIF 378/18. (photo courtesy of Greg VanWyngarden)

U84–85: Two more very poor-quality images that might also have captured D.VIIF 378/18. Udet was posing in front of it with *Lt.* Heinrich Drekmann. (photos courtesy of Jörn Leckscheid)

U85

U86

U86 Blowup

U86, 86 Blowup: The recently-delivered D.VIIF 4253/18 at Ferme du Mont Hussard in late July 1918. (photo courtesy of Greg VanWyngarden)

U87

U87–89: One photo of D.VIIF 4253/18 in the last half of July 1918 and two more of it at Epinoy airfield on 21 August 1918. The first photo offers a rare look at the port side of the airplane (in the background). We are reasonably sure that it was 4253/18 in July because (i) the style and relative positioning of the lettering in "LO!" more closely resemble those seen in U88 than in U84 – i.e., the "L" is closer to the edge and center of the "O", the "!" is lower than the top of the "L" as opposed to being even with it, etc., and (ii) 4253/18 was accepted at Schwerin-Görries on 5 July and the man in the foreground is *Lt.* Heinrich Drekmann, who was killed in action on the 30th of that month. (second photo courtesy of Jörn Leckscheid)

U88

U89

U90–92: These three images originated at *FEA* 2b's airfield near Fürth on 1 or 2 October 1918. Udet had probably flown there on his return trip to the front. They all include D.VIIF 4253/18. (first photo courtesy of Jörn Leckscheid; second courtesy Reinhard Zankl, third photos courtesy of Greg VanWyngarden)

U90

U91

U92

U93

U93: Engineer Kaendler from the Siemens-Schuckert Works is at center talking to Udet in his flight gear at right. Behind them is SSW D.III 8350/17. (photo courtesy of Jack Herris)

U94–95: Two more views of SSW D.III 8350/17 at *Jasta* 4's Metz-Frescaty airfield. (first photo courtesy of Rainer Absmeier; second photo courtesy of Greg VanWyngarden)

U94

U95

U96: Udet signed and dated this picture of him seated in SSW D.III 8350/17.

U96

U97 & 99: Udet strikes two different poses at the nose of SSW D.III 8350/17. (first photo courtesy of Reinhard Zankl)

U98 & 100: Udet in SSW D.III 8350/17 after he had "LO!" painted onto its sides. (first photo courtesy of Greg VanWyngarden)

U100

the "LO!" mark's style more closely resembles the one displayed on Udet's D.VII (OAW) – the machine he was using at the same time as 378/18. Moreover, Udet is standing with *Lt.* Heinrich Drekmann, who was killed in action on 30 July 1918 right when Udet returned from several weeks of leave. Only two D.VIIF aircraft have been associated with Udet prior to that date: his D.VII (OAW) and the newly-arrived 4253/18, which we have eliminated as the subject of these photos.

In any event, Udet did not fly 378/18 for very long because, as already mentioned, he was summoned to Adlershof airfield outside of Berlin in early July to participate in fighter aircraft evaluations being held there and did not return until the end of the month. Accordingly, it is likely that 378/18 was reassigned to another top *Jasta* 4 pilot and repainted during his absence.

Fokker D.VIIF 4253/18
End of July—early October 1918

A Fokker D.VIIF, fitted with BMW engine No.1288, was accepted at the factory on 5 July 1918 and assigned military serial number 4253/18. U86, an image that originated at Ferme du Mont Hussard in late July 1918, tells us that it made it to *Jasta* 4 by the end of the month. U88 shows the same airplane in its full glory on 21 August 1918, when *JG* I units employed Epinoy airfield as a temporary base. Its

factory number, 2954, is visible on the bottom of the rudder. This aircraft was mentioned as Udet's mount in two combat reports for 8 August and 26 September 1918;[23] and U90–92 demonstrate that even after he was slightly wounded on 26 September, he used it on 1 or 2 October, probably on his way back to *JG* I. So he appears to have flown 4253/18 up to the end of the war.

Siemens-Schuckert (SSW) D.III 8350/17
(3–10 October 1918)

Lt. Friedrich Noltenius entered this in his war diary for 6 October 1918: "On this date a French balloon stood for the first time. I had prepared for an attack against it. But prior to it I had a little mock fight with Udet who flew the Siemens D.III with the powerful Remag [*sic* – Rhemag] engine that Udet had brought with him upon returning from leave after being wounded in September. It was impossible to match the performance of this combination."[24] Udet had returned to *Jasta* 4 on 3 October, accompanied by SSW D.III 8350/17 and *Ingenieur* (Engineer) Kaendler from the Siemens-Schuckert Works. Paul Wenzl recalled: "Udet had brought a completely new 'bird' from Mannheim – an 'S.S.W.' (Siemens-Schuckert-Werke) with the new 260-hp S.S.W. rotary engine. The example in this machine made 300 horsepower at 4,000 meters. The machine had been taken up to 8,000 meters, a height it had reached

U101: This enlarged segment comes from the background of a photograph featuring *Lt.* Richard Kraut's Fokker D.VII after he had joined *Jasta* 4 on 3 August 1918. It depicts a SPAD VII from *Escadrille Spa* 62 (note the fighting rooster insignia on the fuselage) that was repainted in German markings and the phrase *"Gute Leute"* ("Good people") applied to its upper wing surface. This is believed to be the SPAD that Udet used for trips behind German lines.(photo courtesy of Greg VanWyngarden)

U102-104: Three pictures of Udet in Fokker D.VIII 238/18 after the war at Fürth airfield. Of particular note is the undercarriage fuel tank that was fitted to the airplane. The external fuel line that carried the fuel to the engine compartment is visible between the undercarriage struts. (photos courtesy of Greg VanWyngarden)

U105

U105: Udet in his red Pfalz D.XV in 1919. (photo courtesy of Greg VanWyngarden)

U106

in 35 minutes. The machine managed 6,000 meters in 10½ to 12 minutes."[25] U93 is a picture of Udet and Kaendler in front of 8350/17 at Metz-Frescaty airfield. U94-95 are two more views of 8350/17 on the airfield. U96 was signed and dated 6 October 1918 by Udet – the same day as his mock dogfight with Noltenius – and U97–98 show him posing at the nose of the aircraft. U99–100 display the airplane after Udet's "LO!" insignia had been applied to the fuselage. That must have occurred fairly soon after

U107

U106–108: In the first image, we see Udet in his red Rumpler D.I D-289 in March 1919. The second and third show D.I D-109 that Udet probably flew as well. (first photo courtesy of Peter M. Bowers Collection, Museum of Flight via Jack Herris; second and third photos courtesy of Greg VanWyngarden)

U108

its arrival because Udet was assigned to *FEA* 3 on 11 October and then sent back to Germany.

SPAD VII
(post-May 1918?)

Jean Edouard Caël, who became a prisoner as a result of Udet's 56th victory on 16 August 1918, wrote in 1920 that when Udet visited him in captivity, he disclosed that "he was going on leave to Munich in a 140-hp SPAD – 'his favorite aircraft' with which he made all of his trips."[26] Udet indeed went home less than a week later and U101 may be a photograph of the airplane that he told Caël he was going to use. It shows a SPAD VII in German

U109

U109–112: These images come from a 1919 event during which Udet was filmed while flying the two-seat Fokker D.VII 10415/18 by the U.S. Signal Corps. Members of the Corps, including a cameraman, can be seen in the first two shots. The third captures Udet about to take off and the fourth has him with a passenger. (photos courtesy of Greg VanWyngarden)

U110

markings with the phrase *"Gute Leute"* ("Good people") in large letters on its upper wing surface. This message certainly suits its use behind German lines since it was obviously intended to notify any German observers that its occupant was friendly. [27] The SPAD also retained its original French unit

U111

U112

insignia – the stylized figure of a rooster in fighting position adopted by *Escadrille Spa* 62. Prior to Udet's leave, SPAD VIIs from that unit were captured on 4 May (*Sous-Lt.* Lucien Gauthier), 5 June (*Sgt.* André Bernard), and 23 June 1918 (*Sgt.* Albert Léon Voisin). *JG* I units can be associated with each of these, but if Bernard turns out to have been Udet's 26th on 5 June

(see page 51 above), then he would seem to be the most logical candidate.

Wartime Aircraft Immediately Postwar

Fokker D.VIII 238/18
   (July/August—12 October 1919)
According to Ishoven, in the summer of 1919 Udet

and Robert *Ritter* von Greim "discovered" some Fokker D.VIIs and D.VIIIs awaiting delivery to the Allies at Bamberg and talked their keeper into letting them "borrow" a few. These are photos of one of them – Fokker D.VIII 238/18 – at what Reinhard Zankl has identified as Fürth airfield. Originally delivered as E.V 238/18 in August 1918, it was redesignated as "D.VIII" after it had been fitted with a redesigned wing. Note the lack of machine guns and the postwar use of an undercarriage fuel tank. Udet and Greim flew their last airshow of the year at Fürth on 12 October 1919.

Pfalz D.XV
(July/August—12 October 1919)

Ishoven said that Udet collected this aircraft at Pfalz's Speyer factory shortly after obtaining his Fokker fighters above, i.e., the summer of 1919. Udet flew the red Pfalz D.XV seen in U105 during airshows and mock dogfights with Robert *Ritter* von Greim.

Rumpler D.I D-289, D.I D-109
(September—12 October 1919)

Udet probably obtained two Rumpler D.I aircraft when he went to work for Rumpler in September 1919. U106 shows him in the cockpit of Rumpler D.I D-289 that another man crashed and destroyed in an airshow held at Augsburg on 5 October 1919. It was painted red and had "Rumpler" in large letters applied to its fuselage. U107–108 captured another Rumpler D.I (D-109) that appears to have been painted red and was probably flown by Udet as well.

Fokker D.VII 10415/18
(1919)

The U.S. Signal Corps filmed Udet flying Fokker D.VII 10415/18 at Kbely Airfield, Prague, in 1919 after it had been converted into a two-seater. U109–112 originated at that time.

Endnotes

[1] *Kreuz wider Kokarde*, p.23.
[2] *Mein Fliegerleben*, p.12.
[3] Herris, *Aviatik Aircraft of WWI*, pp.10-11.
[4] *Mein Fliegerleben*, p.30.
[5] Ibid., p.31.
[6] Various sources have given either *FFA* 48 or *FFA* 68 as *KEK* Habsheim's "parent" unit, and one has stated that it was first attached to *FFA* 48 and later to *FFA* 68.
[7] Grosz, *Pfalz E.I–E.VI*, p.36.
[8] *Mein Fliegerleben*, opposite p.41. The serial number of this D.III is sometimes given as 364/16; but the *Werksnummer* (655) is visible on the interplane struts in U41 and Peter Grosz determined that this was assigned military serial 368/16.
[9] *Fokker Fighters D.I–IV*, p.33. Grosz also names the airfield as "Wynghane" but *Jasta* 15 was never based at Wingene. Udet's subsequent unit, *Jasta* 37, was however, but by the time Udet was with them they were certainly not using a Fokker D.III. The error probably stems from some kind of mixup of the two.
[10] Ishoven, *The Fall of an Eagle* (opposite p.33) provided the date of 1 January 1917 in its caption for this snapshot. The provenance of this information is unknown, however, and such an early date seems unlikely given that 1941/16 would have been the 32nd aircraft in the first batch of D.IIIs (numbered 1910–2316/16) that were delivered, with only 13 having made it to the front by the end of 1916 (see Herris, *Albatros Aircraft of WWI*, Vol.4, p.5). Also, the relatively light clothing the men are wearing does not seem to support the claim that the outside temperature was -20 degrees Celsius (-4 degrees Fahrenheit) when the photo was taken.
[11] Herris, *Albatros Aircraft of WWI*, Vol.4, pp.4–5.
[12] The balloon company responded that they indeed witnessed a dofight at that time, that the Englishman went down suddenly in the direction of Houthem, but they could not see the impact because of trees that were in the way. Udet was not awarded a victory on 9 March 1918.
[13] *Kreuz wider Kokarde*, opposite p.96.
[14] *Mein Fliegerleben*, opposite p.73.
[15] It is clear from the level of detail that Udet provided, that he was referring to his combat report while speaking to Rogers. It is known that Triplanes 144–48/17 and 150–55/17 were delivered to *Jasta* 11 in mid-December 1917 and it seems likely that 149/17 accompanied them (see Leaman, *Fokker Dr.I Triplane*, pp.190–91).
[16] *The Fokker Triplane*, p.96.
[17] Ibid.
[18] Upon close examination, it becomes clear that U73 was edited before being printed. For example, (i) the starboard interplane struts have been drawn in, (ii) the upper wing's dimensions gradually change from left to right, and (iii) the striping on its upper surface is inconsistent in its angles and widths. There is no evidence, however, that the chevron on the horizontal stabilizer was shortened by editing.
[19] *Richthofen Flieger*, p.47.
[20] *Motor* May/June 1919, (photocopy of article without page numbers); article also translated by Alex Imrie in *Cross & Cockade* 2:2, pp.97–99.

145

Udet mentions that he tested his BMW-powered D.VII prior to 1 July 1918. So the "man then in command" was *Lt.* Erich Loewenhardt who temporarily took over *JG* I's reins on 19 June 1918 while *Hptm.* Wilhelm Reinhard was away in Berlin (where he died in a crash on 3 July).

[21] p.48.

[22] Fokker-built D.VII 378/18, powered by BMW engine No.1243, had been accepted at the factory on 15 May before being shipped to the front.

[23] See pp.62 and 65 above and *Mein Fliegerleben*, photos between pp.104 and 105.

[24] *Cross & Cockade* 7:4, pp.334–35.

[25] *Richthofen-Flieger*, p.72.

[26] *La Vie Aérienne*, 5 February 1920, p.944. The original French: "*Il m'annonça qu'il allait partir en permission pour Munich sur un Spad 140 hp 'son appareil préferé' avec lequel il faisait tous ses voyages.*"

[27] We can surmise that the same phrase was probably applied to the underside wing surfaces as well.

Right: Udet and Eleonore "Lo" Zink, who inspired several of Udet's personal markings on his aircraft.

1. Aviatik B.II 1327/15

1. Aviatik B.II 1327/15, *Artillerie-Flieger-Abteilung* **206.** The French aeronautical magazine *L'Aerophile* published a study of captured Aviatik B and C-types, entitled "les Aviatiks 1914–1916". The first section described Aviatik B-types and stated: "All fabric surfaces were linen, doped with Aviatol, an allegedly non-inflammable cellulose acetate varnish." The second section described the Aviatik C.I of 1916 and revealed: "The frame of the wings was covered, as in old-style German machines, in white linen doped with a colorless transparent varnish (resembling cellon)." When the former pilot Professor Kurt H. Weil (who had flown Aviatik B-types when he trained at the Aviatik School in Leipzig-Mockau) was interviewed in 1961, he recalled specifically: "Well, the old Aviatiks were snow white, with sometimes black linings or corners, so we called them 'flying death announcements.'…These aircraft were brilliant white – so white that if you flew in sunlight, they looked transparent from the ground." To this we can add Udet's casual statement about: "Our white Aviatik with the 120 hp Mercedes…"

Thus we can propose that Udet's Aviatik machines in *AFA* 206 were covered in clear-doped white (possibly bleached) fabric, presenting a very pale appearance. From the beginning of 1915, aviation units assigned to *Armee-Abteilung* Gaede were ordered to be decorated with broad black white stripes or "lines" (*Striche*) on the fuselage in addition to their Iron Cross national markings. It is believed that this was initially done in Bavarian *FFA* 8 and *FFA* 9, as those units operated Ago C.I twin-boom machines which could be easily mistaken for French Farman types, and also Pfalz Parasols which were direct copies of French Morane-Saulnier monoplanes. The black/white markings helped German Flak units to identify these aircraft as German machines; the same markings would be applied to other types in *AA* Gaede as well. Photos U3 to U5 show B.II 1327/15 with the stripes applied diagonally and a narrow black border on the leading white stripe. The application of Iron Crosses to the wheel covers was a common Aviatik practice at this time. Note the circular Aviatik decal applied to the center of the rudder cross.

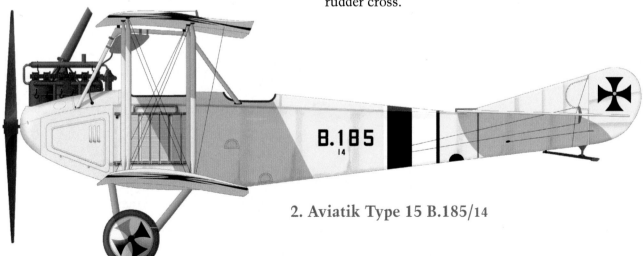

2. Aviatik Type 15 B.185/14

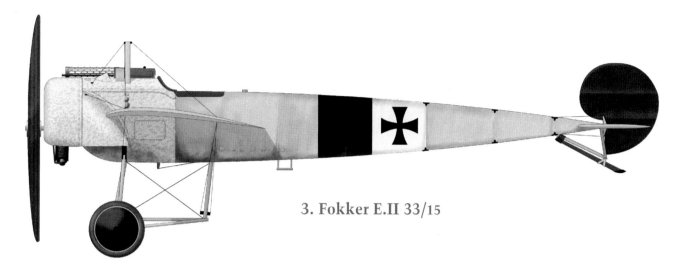

3. Fokker E.II 33/15

2. Aviatik Type 15 B.185/14, *Artillerie-Flieger-Abteilung* 206. On this machine the black/white stripes were applied in a vertical manner and in with the black stripe leading. Once again, the white stripe was given a narrow black border to make it stand out against the white unpainted fabric. Again, the military serial number B.185 was applied to the fuselage in block letters, with the '14' suffix marked below. The translucent qualities of the fabric covering may be noted.

3. Fokker E.II 33/15, *KEK* Habsheim, December 1915. As demonstrated in photos U18 through U21, this Fokker E.II had previously served in *FFA* 9b and displayed the *Armee-Abteilung* Gaede black/white markings. In this case these consisted of vertical bands, with no black border for the white band that served as a background for the Iron Cross emblem. In contrast to E.I 54/15, the Iron Cross national insignia was not repeated on top of the fuselage. In common with several other monoplane fighters in *AA* Gaede,

the rudder has been painted completely black. Photo U18 would certainly indicate that Udet flew it at least once, only to prang it. The underside of the fuselage exhibited considerable staining by the time Udet nosed it over, and the serial number legend on the fuselage had been worn away.

4. Fokker E.III 105/15, *KEK* Habsheim, circa December 1915. Here we have chosen to first portray the port side of this E.III as it appears in photo U22, just after Udet had overturned it on a muddy airfield (apparently with only slight damage that was quickly repaired). At the time of this incident, E.III 105/15 displayed all of the classic black and white markings of *AA* Gaede in brilliant fashion, with both the black and white sashes being bordered in the opposite color. The serial number was clearly visible in a forward position, and the machine exhibited few signs of wear or use. The national cross insignia was applied to the white sash on top of the fuselage as well, and the rudder was painted black.

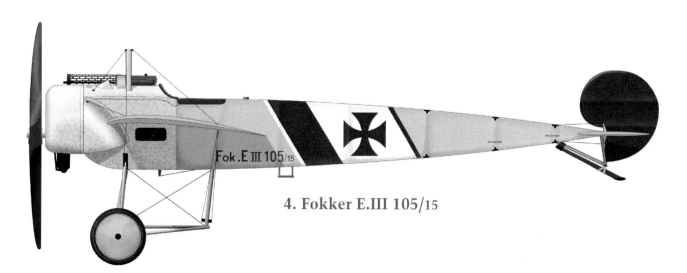

4. Fokker E.III 105/15

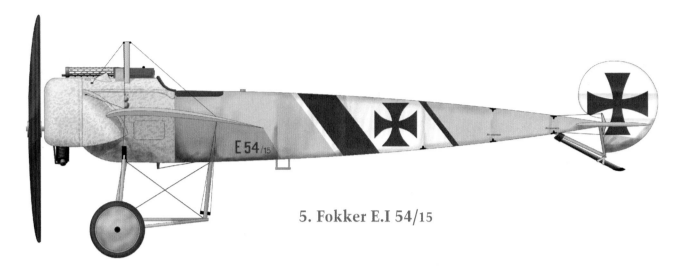

5. Fokker E.I 54/15

5. **Fokker E.I 54/15, *KEK* Habsheim, circa January 1916.** This profile is based on photo U16, and the date is approximate. However, it shows that Udet could have been flying this machine when its black and white *AA* Gaede markings were still intact, as shown in the profile. If the photo was taken in 1916, it must have been quite early in that year before Thomsen's command to remove the black/white markings had been effected. Also, there is no sign of the Egyptian hieroglyph markings, though this photo shows only the port side of the aircraft. The "*Hier unterstützen*" (support here) legend on the aft fuselage is still intact and the aircraft displays a less soiled appearance than it does in U10. As shown in U15, the rudder was white with the usual Iron Cross marking.

6. **Fokker E.I 54/15, *KEK* Habsheim, circa March 1916.** The controversial finish of the Fokker *Eindecker* fighters has been discussed frequently in previous volumes in this series. In period photos, the wings and fuselages of these aircraft consistently display a darker and more opaque finish than contemporary German two-seaters that were covered in clear-doped white linen. The bulk of available documentary evidence indicates that the Fokker fabric produced an opaque beige, yellowish or light brown appearance. A report on Fokkers in *L'Aerophile* stated specifically that: "… the fabric of the Fokker wings was generally of beige color in 1916." Most Fokker photos indicate that the monoplanes had degrees of soiling from the oil thrown out by the engine, which soaked through the fabric from the inside out. The longer an aircraft was in service, the greater the degree of soiling. This soiling did not seem to penetrate through the painted white fields of the cross insignia in the same way. This indicates that the fabric was left unpainted. The fairly extensive report on the captured E.III 210/16 makes no mention at all of the color of the fabric and only states that it was "coarse". This would point to the possibility of Fokker using a considerably coarser, more opaque fabric than most other German manufacturers. As pointed out in

6. Fokker E.I 54/15

the main text, Udet's E.I 54/15 had previously been painted with the black and white sash markings of aircraft in *Armee-Abteilung* Gaede. However, again as noted in the text, the leading sash color, as well as the trailing border of the white sash, clearly did not seem to be black when photos U9 through U14 were taken. Many suggestions for the mysterious color of these markings have been made over the years, with red and blue being most popular. Blue was suggested because Udet was actually a Bavarian – but *KEK* Habsheim was a Prussian unit, and Udet was never fiercely nationalistic about his Bavarian origins. The light tonality of the sash as seen in the photos certainly does not indicate it could have been

red. As author Lance Bronnenkant has noted, it is most likely that the original black markings were simply overpainted in an attempt to match the beige fuselage finish. At the end of 1915, the *Feldflugchef* Hermann Thomsen ordered that the black/white markings were to be removed from the aircraft of *AA* Gaede; this is likely what led to the obliteration of the black portions of the sash markings, leaving only the white backgrounds for the Iron Cross insignia. Even more intriguing than the sash marking is the application of the Egyptian hieroglyphs of the *djed*, *ankh*, and *was*. The reason for their use is unknown, but they perhaps are one of many indications of Udet's artistic talents and proclivity.

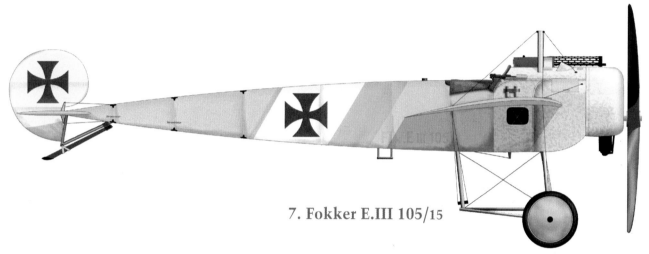

7. Fokker E.III 105/15

7. Fokker E.III 105/15, *KEK* Habsheim, early 1916.
By the time photos U23 through U31 were exposed, the black portions of the *AA* Gaede markings had been painted over, in a style very similar to that seen on E.I 54/15. We presume that this was in a color approximating the beige of the fuselage fabric. The Iron Cross markings in the remaining white sash on both the sides and top of the fuselage were retained, although photos U28 through U30 show that the cross on the port side was seriously degraded or smudged. The once-black rudder was either painted white or recovered completely, and a new Iron Cross emblem of small proportions was applied by the unit. One very interesting aspect of the plane at this time was the installation of a P08 Luger pistol complete with shoulder stock, which was affixed to the starboard side of the cockpit along with a rack for signal flare cartridges. Udet's exploits at *KEK* Habsheim had already earned him the local nickname of 'the Vosges Sparrow,' according to Alex Imrie.

8. Fokker E.III 404/15, *KEK* Habsheim, early 1916.
This profile illustrates this aircraft as it appears in

photo U33, which shows it at an intermediate stage between U32 and U34. At the time of U33, the Iron Cross emblem on the rudder was again, of small proportions. A narrow, black-bordered white band was painted on the rear fuselage aft of the national insignia, and the military serial number was painted in the usual location. An anemometer device was fitted on the leading edge of the port wing. Close study of U32 and U34 will reveal the subtle changes in markings that this aircraft underwent.

9. Fokker D.III 368/16, *Jasta* 15, November 1916.
Photos U40 and U41 show Udet's famous Fokker D.III 368/16 (w/n 655), which was fitted with a sheet metal profile of "*der stille Beobachter*" (the silent observer) to produce an illusion of a two-seater with a "sting in the tail" to his opponents. A report published in *L'Aerophile*, based on Fokker D.II 536/16 of *Oblt.* Otto Dessloch of *KEK* Ensisheim (which was forced to land in Switzerland on 13 October 1916) stated that: "The wings, fuselage and tail are painted green and brown, and the underside of the wings in light sky blue." We can presume that Udet's D.III 368/16 was finished similarly. The

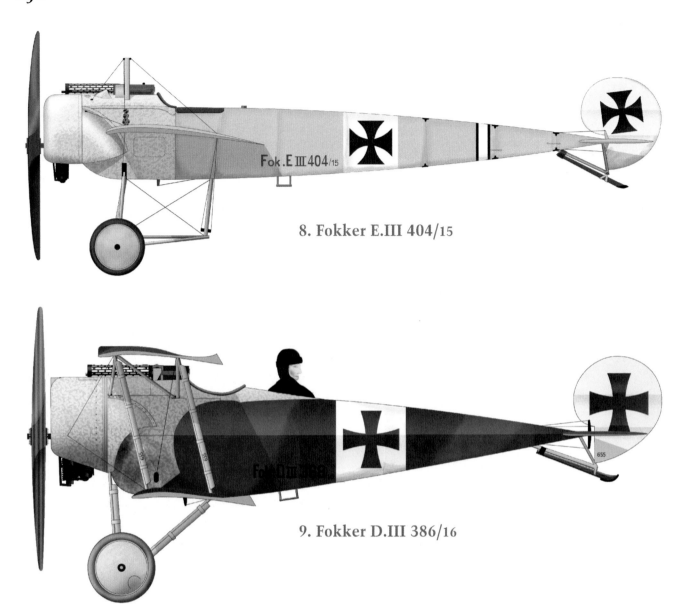

8. Fokker E.III 404/15

9. Fokker D.III 386/16

green and brown shades met in hazy demarcation lines, indicating they may have been sprayed on. The works number 655 was stenciled on the interplane struts, along with other legends.

10. Albatros D.III 1941/16, *Jasta* 15, January 1917. The frequently-published photo U43 famously shows Udet with what was probably his first Albatros D.III in January 1917. This photo, while familiar, presents some enigmatic aspects. The fuselage and fin appear rather dark, and it has been presumed that this indicates that these plywood-covered portions were given a reddish-brown stain (somewhat lighter than the reddish-brown camouflage paint on the wings), as was reportedly carried out on some Albatros D.I and D.II aircraft. However, the white border of the fuselage cross is distinctly subdued or repressed; it is possible the staining was "washed over" the white

cross border and black cross as well (but that is not confirmed). The wings were finished with a three-color camouflage on the upper surfaces, consisting of dark olive green, pale Brunswick green and dark Venetian Red (reddish or chestnut brown). The undersides of the wings were very pale blue; the same camouflage colors were applied to the tailplane surfaces. The rudder exhibits a very dark appearance, and was probably painted in either dark olive green or Venetian Red.

11. Albatros D.V, *Jasta* 37, August 1917. According to the late Alex Imrie, the Albatros D.V pictured in photos U45 through U48 was one of a rather small batch of D.V machines given an overall matt silver finish, much like that applied to Pfalz fighters. This finish extended to the wings as well as the fuselage. A few of these silver Albatros seem to have gone to

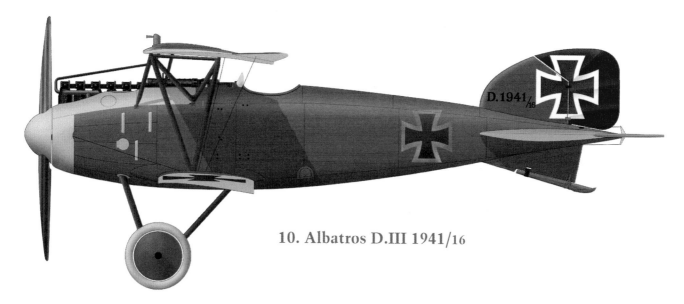

10. Albatros D.III 1941/16

Jasta 37 and possibly to *Jasta* 15. The dark-colored metal cowling panels and struts are presumed to have been black. Udet's D.V was further painted with the *Jasta* 37 unit marking of diagonal black and white stripes on the tailplane/elevator, as instituted by Grasshoff (the unit's first D.III aircraft – seen in U50 – displayed personal markings only on the fuselage, but the unit marking was soon added). The wheel covers of this silver D.V were also white with a single black stripe. While not confirmed, there is

a possibility that the diagonal application of the tail stripes was (in addition to being a very distinctive *Staffel* marking) an early attempt at an "optical illusion" effect to throw off the aim of a pursuer, mandated by Grasshoff. Leader's streamers trailed from the elevator of this silver D.V, presumably indicating Udet was a *Kette* leader even before he was the unit commander. As indicated elsewhere, this may have been the very first of Udet's aircraft to display the famous "LO" emblem.

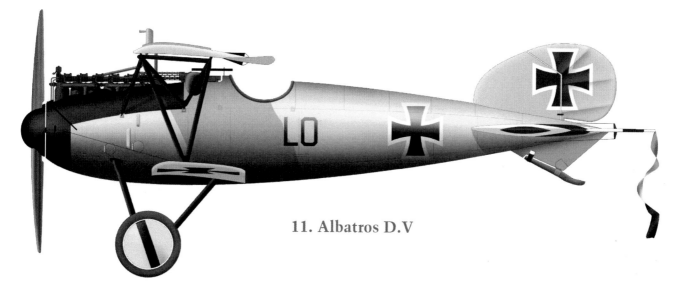

11. Albatros D.V

12. Albatros D.V 4476/17, *Jasta* 37, September 1917. One of the best-photographed and (apparently) long-serving of Udet's Albatros fighters, this D.V displayed the usual 'yellowish' varnished plywood-covered fuselage. The *Staffel* markings in evidence include the black/white diagonal stripes on the tailplane and elevator, and the black spinner. As

noted in the photo captions for U52, this aircraft eventually displayed some cockade bullet hole patches, apparently in RFC colors. The wings and rudder were covered in five-color printed camouflage fabric. This machine was fitted with a rack for flare cartridges on the starboard side of the cockpit, and Udet's usual leader's streamers on the elevator. As

12. Albatros D.V 4476/17

noted in the captions for U57–U59, it seems that this D.V was also marked with Udet's "U" initial in white on the bottom surface of the lower port wing, in order to facilitate recognition of his machine by ground observers. Udet's well-known black Albatros D.Va (next profile) may not have displayed the white "U" in that location, contrary to what has been previously thought.

13. Albatros D.Va, *Jasta* 37, Winter 1917–1918. This profile is based on photos U60–U66. When Udet took command of *Jasta* 37 in November 1917, he introduced a new addition to the *Staffel* markings; from now on, in addition to the distinctive black/white diagonal tail stripes, each machine would display a black fuselage, wheel covers and struts. Each pilot was identified by a white personal number on the nose (from 1–14, omitting unlucky 13) and this number was often repeated on the underside of one or both lower wings (in black on

light blue undersides, in black on 'lozenge' fabric). Each pilot also employed a large fuselage symbol, usually white, which appeared between the cross and cockpit. In place of the usual nose number, Udet utilized a white chevron on the nose of his black D.Va as a leader's emblem – a marking he would repeat on some of his later machines. Udet's familiar 'LO' badge appeared on the fuselage in white block letters. In addition to the chevron and streamers from the elevator, Udet employed two chordwise white stripes on the top surface of the upper wing, inboard of the crosses, to further identify the *Staffel* commander's plane. This D.Va was fitted with a wind-driven generator on the leading starboard undercarriage strut, and a rack for six flare cartridges on the starboard side of the cockpit. It has long been believed that this black Albatros was additionally marked with a full-chord white "U" on the underside of the lower port wing, in place of the numbers which appeared on other machines of the

13. Albatros D.Va

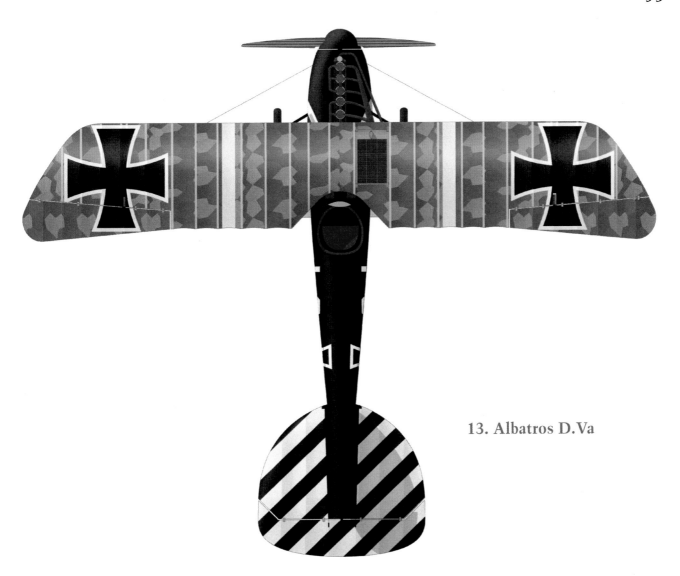

13. Albatros D.Va

unit .However, photos U57 and U58, which were taken by a two-seater observer flying above Udet as he looped his Albatros, seem to show a varnished yellow fuselage, and photo U59 shows the white "U" on the wing of D.V 4476/17. The presence of a white "U" on the lower wing of his black Albatros D.Va is a question which awaits further evidence.

14. Fokker Dr.I 586/17, *Jasta* 4, late May 1918. As explained in the text and shown in photos U69–U74, Udet acquired this spectacularly decorated machine of Hans Kirschstein of *Jasta* 6 when some of that unit's triplanes were handed off to *Jasta* 4. Kirschstein's similarly-marked Fokker D.VII was called *die optische Taeuschung* (the optical illusion) and we can probably assume that this Dr.I was similarly named, as its disruptive diagonal stripes were intended to throw off the aim of an enemy. The stripes on the top of the upper wing were repeated on the underside of that wing, while the stripes on

the fuselage angled in different directions on the two sides of the fuselage. The middle and bottom wings retained their factory camouflage. According to *Jasta* 6 pilot Richard Wenzl, these black and white "dazzle" markings were so effective, Kirschstein's aircraft was only ever hit in the port wing. The *Jasta* 6 unit marking of chordwise stripes on the tailplane/ elevators were retained unaltered, as was the black cowling of the unit (most other *Jasta* 4 Dr.I's featured 'off-white', possibly pale blue cowlings). The wheel covers were halved in black/white, a detail just discernible in some of the photos. There were rectangular access panels on both sides just aft of the cowling, and just ahead of the carburetor air intake, another *Jasta* 6 hallmark. It would appear that the only modification Udet made was to apply his "LO" marking to both fuselage sides in block letters – probably in red to contrast with the black stripes. By the time this machine was photographed at Cramoiselle, it showed noticeable signs of wear

14. Fokker Dr.I 586/17

and oil staining, which slightly subdued the disparity between the black and white stripes of the small photos in the Oskar Rouselle album.

15. Fokker Dr.I 593/17, *Jasta 4*, **circa June 1918.** Udet probably flew this Dr.I for only a brief period, after 586/17 suffered a detached cylinder in flight. Shown in photos U75–U77, this Dr.I remained mostly in

the factory camouflage finish, with open-ended *Balkenkreuz* insignia in all locations. It is possible that the cowling, struts and wheels were eventually painted in the unit's "off-white" *Staffel* markings, but our few poor-quality and blemished photos do not reveal such décor at the time they were taken. The struts may have been undersurface blue, or else a dark solid olive. Udet had drawn out a very small

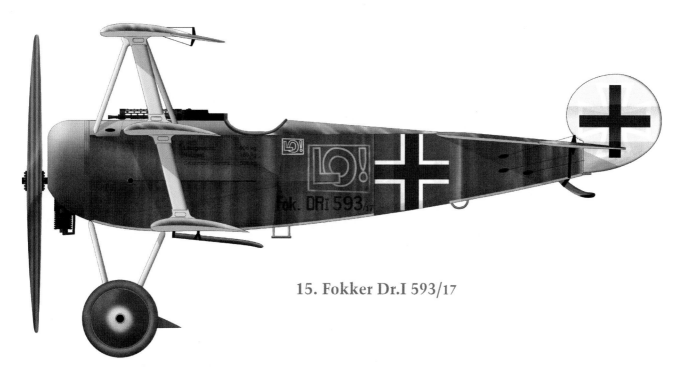

15. Fokker Dr.I 593/17

"thumbnail sketch" of a new version of his "LO" marking on the upper side of the fuselage aft of the cockpit; this was done either in chalk or white paint. For the first time, the "L" intersected the "O" of the marking, and an exclamation point was added – all within a small square. This was intended to serve as a model for the *Staffel* painter to apply it in much larger form on the fuselage ahead of the national insignia. It certainly appears that – at the time of the photos – this larger version of the insignia had been lightly chalked on in preparation for the permanent paint job. Whether this was actually ever completed remains unknown. What is certain from photo U77 is that Udet identified his plane with a white leader's chevron, just as he had on his black *Jasta* 37 D.Va (and possibly on his *Jasta* 11 Dr.I 149/17, as explained in the caption to photo U68). The chevron was painted on to the tailplane and elevator, most likely against a standard factory finish, and was large enough that his pilots could easily see it in the air. This prefigured the identical insignia that would be painted on to at least two of his later Fokker D.VIIs. Incidentally, the historian Alex Imrie speculated that the new version of the "LO" emblem, with intertwined letters and an exclamation point, may have signified an "even closer tie" with his fiancée Eleonore Zink.

16. Fokker D.VII (OAW) *Jasta* 4, June 1918. This is the most famous and iconic of all of Udet's WWI aircraft – yet its actual full appearance remains controversial. Though it has been depicted in

paintings, models, and replicas countless times, it must be emphasized that all of these interpretations are based on only one halftone photo from *Mein Fliegerleben*, taken on 28 June, in which Udet's figure obscures most of the aircraft and which was heavily retouched for publication. Thus, a lot of speculation has always gone into portrayals of this short-lived aircraft. *Jasta* 4 received its first batch of Fokker D.VIIs, all of them built under license by OAW on 13 June 1918. These all came from the first OAW production batch numbered 2000/18 – 2199/18 (2063/18 and 2077/18 are documented at *Jasta* 4, so the first consignment of D.VIIs to *Jasta* 4 were likely in the 206x/18 and 207x/18 range) and were equipped with Mercedes engines. The aircraft seen in the classic photo U78 was no doubt one of these, though its specific serial remains unknown. From the retouched photo, we can see that the tailplane and elevator of this D.VII were painted a dark color and the *"Du doch nicht!!"* legend and Udet's usual leader's chevron were applied in white. Prior to this point, Udet had never used a largely-red aircraft (though his Dr.I in *Jasta* 11 would have had some red markings). Only five days after this photo was taken, Udet's replacement Fokker was seen by *Jasta* 66 ace Werner Preuss during a dogfight above the Forest of Villers-Cotterêts. He saw that planes of *JG* I were engaging several formations of Spads, and witnessed one that was: "… Pursued by two Frenchmen…I recognize a red machine . . . Udet!!" To this author, this indicates that even by 3 July, Udet was already well-known for flying a red Fokker by pilots of

16. Fokker D.VII

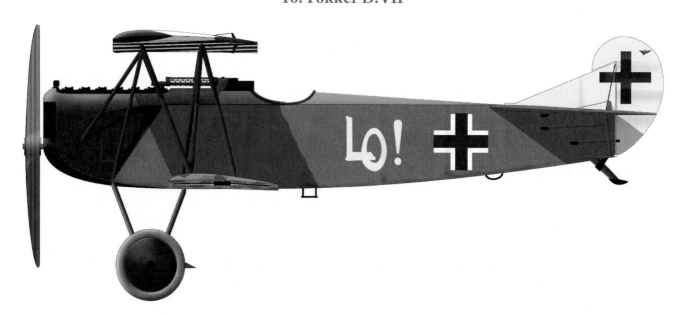

nearby units. So, it is likely that the tailplane and fuselage of the "*Du doch nicht!!*" D.VII was also red. Having flown under Richthofen and witnessed how readily a red color scheme made a plane identifiable for victory confirmation, Udet had selected this color which would be identified with him from then on (even into the post-war years). Udet had just mandated a new unit marking for *Jasta* 4 in the form of black noses, wheels and struts. We have chosen to depict Udet's first red D.VII as employing these unit markings, though that remains speculative. The white shape visible in the crook of Udet's right arm in the photo (a subject of intense discussion by enthusiasts) is almost certainly merely an artifact of the retouching process and nothing more. The upper surfaces of the lower wings retained the standard four-color printed camouflage fabric with light colored (probably natural linen) rib tapes. The undersides of the bottom wing were probably also in printed fabric in the undersurface pattern. The most striking and oft-discussed aspect of this aircraft are the distinctive white and dark stripes on the top surface of the upper wing, of course. These have traditionally been depicted as red and white, but it is our opinion that they were more likely black and white as shown. Udet had direct experience with these "optical illusion" markings on the black/white striped Dr.I 586/17 (and, incidentally, on the tails of his *Jasta* 37 Albatros fighters) and used them on his first D.VII for a similar purpose. Such stripes required a good deal of effort to apply, and were intended to deflect the aim of a pursuing opponent through disruption. Such diagonal striping would be employed by a number of German *Jagdflieger*, such as Kirschstein, Neckel, and Rumey. The famous black/white *Jasta* 5 striped D.VII (OAW) 4598/18 flown by Könnecke and Mai is another example,

and a similar D.VII was used in *Jasta* 52. The colors used for such 'illusion' stripes were always black and white – which, of course, provided the greatest contrast. For these reasons we have chosen to depict the stripes on Udet's D.VII as black/white; close inspection of the photo in *Mein Fliegerleben* does reveal that the national insignia cross partially visible on the starboard wing did indeed have a white border. The precise number and pattern of these stripes remains a problematic matter to ascertain; also, we cannot say with certainty if the stripes were repeated on the underside of the top wing, or not. The form of 'LO!' marking depicted, and the style of fuselage cross, is speculative. No doubt many readers will have their own opinions about the appearance of this celebrated D.VII, but this is our interpretation at this time. (see Appendix on page 171 below for greater details)

17. Fokker D.VII (OAW), Jasta 4, July–August 1918.
This profile is based on the D.VII seen in photos U79 to U82, which apparently depict Udet's reserve, Mercedes-engined Fokker during this period. It is possible that he employed this machine as a reserve for his much-preferred BMW-engined D.VIIs, for when he led the pilots of his *Staffel* in their Mercedes D.VIIs in formation flights. This OAW-built aircraft largely retained its finish of four-color printed fabric. As is evident, it was marked with Udet's usual "LO!" emblem in white and his favored white command chevron on the lozenge-fabric tailplane and elevator The black nose, struts, and wheel cover unit markings of *Jasta* 4 are clearly in use on this D.VII. The fin and rudder of this OAW-built Fokker were covered in clear-doped, unpainted linen, as were those of his "*Du doch nicht!!*" D.VII. The colored fuselage borders on the longeron

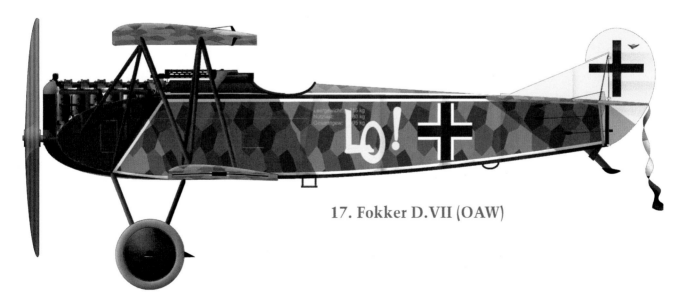

17. Fokker D.VII (OAW)

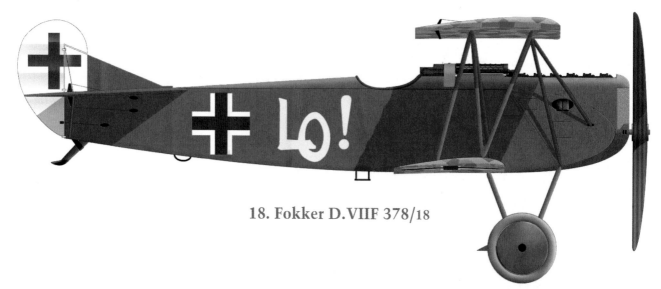

18. Fokker D.VIIF 378/18

positions were a common feature of many *Jasta* 4 D.VIIs. According to historian Bruno Schmäling, these were seemingly in different colors selected by each pilot; Udet's are interpreted as black with white outlines. As usual, black and white *Staffelführer* streamers trailed from the elevator. This author is deeply indebted to D.VII historian Jörn Leckscheid for his insights on this and all of Udet's D.VIIs.

18. Fokker D.VIIF 378/18 (w/n 2465), July 1918.

Udet's first BMW-engined D.VIIF was acquired just a few days before he was shot down on 29 June. He revealed the serial number to journalist David B. Rogers circa 1931, when he referred to his combat report in describing his fight with a French Breguet on 1 July 1918. The captions for photos U83–U85 explain why those photos almost certainly show D.VIIF 378/18, with factory number 2465 and BMW IIIa 1243. It was accepted at the Fokker Factory on 15 May and could have reached *JG* I by 22 June, when the first BMW Fokkers arrived. It was in use at the same time as the 'lozenge' fabric D.VII (OAW) in the previous profile, and the style of "LO!" insignia is somewhat similar (and quite different from that seen on 4253/18). Udet shot down Wanamaker flying this plane, on 2 July, and Wanamaker recalled: "I suddenly discovered that a red Fokker was pouring lead into my plane." This is also the "red machine" recognized by Preuss on 3 July, and was red on the fuselage and tail. It is our belief that Udet did not bother with sticking with the black nose, struts and wheel markings of *Jasta* 4 on this aircraft, but rather it is likely that all of these components were red. In his article "My Experiences with the B.M.W. Motor Type IIIa," Udet wrote: "At first 22 [BMW] were delivered to *Jasta* 11...I quickly obtained two of these crates from the man then in command;"

this points to the possibility that the two machines Udet "wangled" were already painted in *Jasta* 11 red markings. With red nose, fuselage, and tail this D.VII was easy for his comrades to recognize, and also facilitated confirmation of his victories. The "exception to the rule" was justified; Udet generally flew this machine only in the company of Drekmann, so identification as a *Jasta* 4 machine was unnecessary. Whether or not the white chevron was applied to the tail surfaces cannot be determined from available photos. The wings most likely remained in their printed fabric finish, possibly four-color (D.VII 379/18 was definitely covered in four-color fabric, while 382/18 and 406/18 had five-color). The works number 2465 was likely inscribed on one side of the base of the rudder. This D.VII was fitted with one of the early collector-style exhausts that exited through the side cowling panel.

19. Fokker D.VIIF 4253/18 (w/n 2954), August-October 1918.

This is the most well-documented and successful of all of Udet's D.VIIs. It was accepted on 5 July and had BMW IIIa 1288. Works number 2954 was marked at the base of the white rudder on the starboard side only, just below the Fokker trademark, and these were repeated at the base of the white portion of the fin, next to the rudder post. It was fitted with a 'saxophone' type exhaust, and the upper cowling panels were removed. Udet's combat report for 8 August described the "red fuselage, with the letters 'LO' on both sides and two streamers on the elevator." His report for 26 September similarly recorded the red fuselage. The appended witness statements to that report also mentioned "the red machine of *Lt*. Udet" (Göring), "the bright red machine of *Lt*. Udet" (von Wedel, *Jasta* 11), "a red Fokker" (von Boenigk, *JG* II), "the red machine"

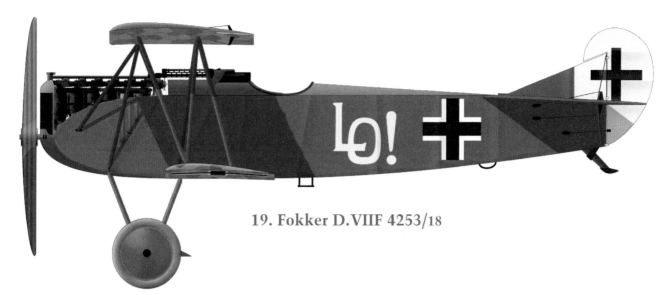

19. Fokker D.VIIF 4253/18

(v. Radzack, *Lt.*), and "The red aircraft was easily recognizable from the ground" (Koepsch, *Jasta* 4). Such corroboration provides ample evidence of Udet's reasons for his choice of color scheme. The nose, struts, wheel covers and both surfaces of the tailplane were red. The bottom wing was covered in four-color fabric with dark (pink?) rib tapes, and full-chord *Balkenkreuz* insignia were employed. A very small white serial number is just discernible on the underside of the port aileron of the top wing in photo U90. This and other factors indicate that the upper wing seen in photos U88 to U92 was a replacement component from an OAW-built D.VII. The number is not clearly legible, but it may read "Fok. D7 (O.A.W.) 2076." The crosses on the upper wing, visible in U88, were not full chord and did not extend to the ailerons – another hallmark of early OAW D.VIIs. Furthermore, close study of the photos reveal no evidence of printed camouflage polygons or contrasting rib tapes on the top of the upper wing; therefore, it is the opinion of Jörn Leckscheid and the authors that the upper surface of the top wing was also painted red. Udet and the BMW D.VII were a perfect match, and he gained his last 22 victories in this machine – often while flying alone. Richard Wenzl wrote: "Most of the time, Udet flew at high altitude far behind the lines and in this way surprised many unsuspecting 'lone wanderers,' as they flew homeward." A relevant letter taken from a French POW was circulated in the September *Nachrichtenblatt*: "A comrade was attacked twice while at 5,000 meters and within our lines…The second time by a single Fokker which was painted red all over quite far behind our lines. Despite all manner of aerobatics by our pilot…the Fokker did not relent from 5,000 to 3,000 meters and fired his machine guns at our man from the somewhat great distance of 150–200 meters and put 30 holes into [our] crate. …The machine had to be dismantled… Furthermore, this red-painted machine has been talked about several times recently. In any event, in it sits a pilot equal to our Fonck." Udet himself described his tactics when he met René Fonck in 1928: "I used to wait until night was about to fall and then, flying at a height of 15,000 to 18,000 feet, I would get behind your lines, turn my tail toward the setting sun, and wait for your machines to return home. With the sun in their eyes they were easy to pick off."

20. Siemens-Schuckert (SSW) D.III 8350/17, October 1918. Udet brought this SSW with him upon his return from leave, but it was only at the front from 3 to 10 October; he likely did very little operational flying in it. Nonetheless it was an object of great interest and photos U93 through U100 record its changing appearance. Joseph Doerflinger was an enlisted pilot who served briefly in *Jastas* 10 and 4, and many years later he wrote: "Udet, as I knew him, was an active little fellow, full of life and fun…I remember it well that it was at Metz that Udet received a brand new Siemens-Schuckert plane which he immediately painted red. Then he painted his sweetheart's initials on it. I remember him telling me how much this delighted her…Our flying was nothing to the show Udet gave us in his new plane…He looped, he stood vertically on a wing and did some of the strangest curves." As evident from photos U94 to U96, initially the fuselage and horizontal tail surfaces were red with no "LO!" insignia. Eventually as seen in U98 and U100, he had his usual emblem added – at least on the starboard side – so the photographers could record it. Some enthusiasts have suggested that the upper surfaces

20. SSW D.III 8350/17

of the wings were also painted red. However, the views in U94 and U98 distinctly reveal the printed camouflage fabric on the lower wing, and it is most likely the wings remained in factory finish. We would like to thank SSW authority Dick Bennett for his help with this aircraft.

21. Pfalz D.XV, September–October 1919. We have chosen to illustrate a couple of the 1918-era aircraft that Udet flew in displays in Bavaria in 1919, as they were WWI types. We have limited our coverage to 1919, as to profile and illustrate all of the aircraft Udet flew from 1919 until his death

would require several more books. In the summer of 1919 Udet and his friend Robert *Ritter* von Greim were searching for aircraft in hopes of flying in some airshows. Finally they found a group of Fokker D.VIIs and D.VIIIs awaiting delivery to the Allies in Bamberg, and managed to 'acquire' a few of these. At this same time, Udet visited the Pfalz Works in Speyer where he was presented with a new Pfalz D.XV. Artist Ludwig Hohlwein designed the posters reproduced in this book, showing Udet's all-red Fokker D.VIII parasol. In their first airshow on 11 August in Munich, Udet flew a Fokker D.VII, D.VIII, and his Pfalz D.XV, all bright red. On 21

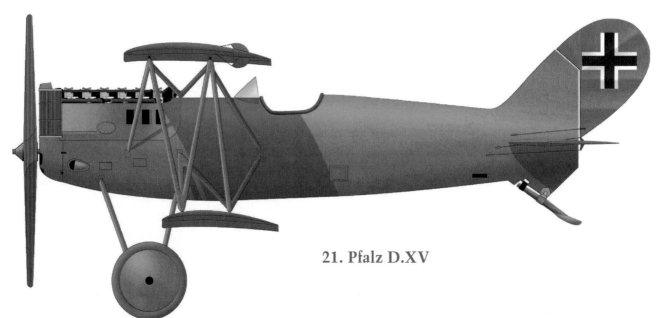

21. Pfalz D.XV

22. Rumpler D.I D289

August, they performed again at Tegernsee. Profile 21 shows Udet's all-red Pfalz D.XV, as seen in photo U105. That photo was reportedly taken during an attempt by Udet to set a new world altitude record; at that time, the rudder and wings still retained their *Balkenkreuz* insignia. Later during the airshows in August, all national markings had been painted over. In 1922 Udet sold the D.XV to former *Jasta* 16b pilot Max Holtzem, who was flying as an exhibition pilot in Argentina. Holtzem had the D.XV converted to a two-seater for passenger flights.

22. **Rumpler D.I D-289.** On 25 September, Udet got his private pilot's license and was officially employed at the Bavarian Rumpler Works in Augsburg. He acquired a Rumpler D.I D-289 and it was naturally painted all red, with the serial number in a lighter color and "Rumpler" emblazoned on the fuselage. On 5 October 1919 at an airshow at Augsburg, Udet flew his all-red D-289 while von Greim flew a silver Rumpler. After most of the flying was over, the parachutist/pilot Tony Ficklscherer decided to fly Udet's Rumpler D-289. He crashed fatally and destroyed the aircraft. This is probably why Udet later had another Rumpler D.I, D109, which he flew at Fürth on 12 October 1919 in the last performance of this duo. It too was painted red.

Ernst Udet – Military Service

Significant Dates

26 Apr 1896	Born in Frankfurt am Main
18 Aug 1914	Volunteer motorcyclist for *26. Reserve-Division* (Württemberg)
15 Sep 1914	Posted to Strasbourg military government
25 Sep 1914	Began stay at *Kraftwagenpark* Namur
20 Oct 1914	Released from volunteer service
late Apr 1915	Obtained civilian pilot's license
15 Jun 1915	*Flieger* with *Flieger-Ersatz-Abteilung 9*
4 Sep 1915	Assigned to *Artillerie-Flieger-Abteilung 206*
21 Sep 1915	Promoted to *Gefreiter*
2 Oct 1915	Sent to *Armee-Flug-Park* Gaede
28 Nov 1915	Promoted to *Unteroffizier*
29 Nov 1915	Assigned to *Kampfeinsitzer-Kommando* Habsheim
13 Mar 1916	Promoted to *Vizefeldwebel*
18 Mar 1916	First victory
8 Oct 1916	Member of *Jagdstaffel* 15
17 Oct 1916	Designated *Fähnrich*
5 Nov 1916	Promoted to *Offizier-Stellvertreter*
22 Jan 1917	Promoted to *Leutnant*
5 Aug 1917	Assigned to *Jagdstaffel* 37
7 Nov 1917	CO of *Jagdstaffel* 37
24 Mar 1918	Acting CO of *Jagdstaffel* 11
9 Apr 1918	Aawarded *Pour le Mérite*
17 Apr 1918	Officially posted to *Jagdgeschwader Nr.I's Jasta* 11 (backdated to 5 April)
22 May 1918	CO of *Jagdstaffel* 4
11 Sep 1918	Promoted to *Oberleutnant*
26 Sep 1918	Final victory (# 62)
26 Sep 1918	Wounded in action
11 Oct 1918	Assigned to *Flieger-Ersatz-Abteilung 3*
--------------	--------------
10 Jan 1919	Released from military service
1919	Employed by Gustav Otto Werke
11 Aug 1919	Flew in first show for German POW charity
Sep 1919	Employed by Bayerische Rumpler-Werke
25 Feb 1920	Married Eleonore Zink
23 Oct 1922	Started Udet-Flugzeugbau
16 Feb 1923	Divorced Eleonore Zink
1925	Sold interest in Udet-Flugzeugbau
1928	*Hals und Beinbruch* published
early 1929	Flew for movie *Die weisse Hölle vom Piz Palü*
early 1930	Flew for movie *Stürme über dem Mont Blanc*
late 1930	Flew for movie *Fremde Vögel über Afrika*

late 1932	Flew for movie *S.O.S. Eisberg*
1 May 1933	Joined *Nationalsozialistische Deutsche Arbeiterpartei* (*NSDAP*)
late 1934	Flew for movie *Wunder des Fliegens*
1935	*Mein Fliegerleben* published
1 Jun 1935	Entered Luftwaffe as *Oberst*
1 Sep 1935	Assigned to *Reichsluftfahrtministerium* (*RLM*)
1 Oct 1935	Promoted to *Oberstleutnant*
10 Feb 1936	Named *Inspekteur der Jagd- und Sturzkampfflieger*
10 Jun 1936	Named *Chef des Technischen Amtes*
1 Apr 1937	Promoted to *Generalmajor*
1 Nov 1938	Promoted to *Generalleutnant*
30 Jan 1939	Given title of *Generalluftzeugmeister*
1 Apr 1940	Promoted to *General der Flieger*
July 1940	Promoted to *Generaloberst*
17 Nov 1941	Committed suicide
22 Nov 1941	Buried in Invalidenfriedhof, Berlin

WWI Service Units

18 Aug—14 Sep 1914	*26. Reserve-Division* (Württemberg)
15—24 Sep 1914	Strasbourg military government
25 Sep—20 Oct 1914	*Kraftwagenpark* Namur
15 Jun—3 Sep 1915	*Flieger-Ersatz-Abteilung 9*
4 Sep—1 Oct 1915	*Artillerie-Flieger-Abteilung 206*
2 Oct—28 Nov 1915	*Armee-Flug-Park* Gaede
29 Nov 1915—27 Sep 1916	*Kampfeinsitzer-Kommando* Habsheim
8 Oct 1916—4 Aug 1917	*Jagdstaffel* 15
5 Aug 1917—23 Mar 1918	*Jagdstaffel* 37
24 Mar—20 May 1918	*Jagdstaffel* 11
21 May—26 Sep 1918	*Jagdstaffel* 4
11 Oct—11 Nov 1918	*Flieger-Ersatz-Abteilung 3*

WWI Awards

24 Sep 1915	Iron Cross, 2nd Class – Prussia
20 Mar 1916	Iron Cross, 1st Class – Prussia
17 Oct 1916	*Ehrenbecher* – Germany
4 Nov 1916	Merit Cross with Swords -- Württemberg
13 Nov 1917	Royal Hohenzollern House Order, Knight's Cross with Swords – Prussia
9 Apr 1918	*Pour le Mérite* – Prussia
24 Aug 1918	Hanseatic Cross – Lübeck
17 Sep 1918	Hanseatic Cross – Hamburg
post-26 Sep 1918	Wound Badge in Silver – Germany

Victory List

No.	Date	Aircraft	Location, Unit & Crew*
1	18 Mar 1916	Farman MF 11	Over Mulhouse – *Esc MF* 29: *MdL.* Edouard Albert Joseph Leroy, *Capt.* Emile Victor Bacon (b-KIA)
2	12 Oct	Breguet-Michelin IV No.229	Near Rustenhart – *Esc BM* 120 – *Cpl.* René Bouet (POW), *Sol.* Marcel Delcroix (WIA/POW)
3	24 Dec	Caudron G4	Near Aspach-le-Haut – *Esc C* 34: *MdL.* Jean Joseph Edouard Julien Hourcade, *Sous-Lt.* Louis Napoléon Lombart (b-KIA)
4	20 Feb 1917	Nieuport	Near Aspach – *Esc N* 81: *MdL.* Pierre de Casenove de Pradines (OK)
5	24 Apr	Nieuport	Near Chavignon – ?
6	5 May	SPAD VII	Near Bois de Ville [La Ville-aux-Bois-lès-Pontavert?]– ?
7	14 Aug	DH.4 A2159	Near Pont-à-Vendin – RFC 25: 2Lt. PL McGavin, 2Lt. N Field (b-KIA)
8	15 Aug	Sopwith Strutter A1079.B6	Between Harnes and Loison-sous-Lens – RFC 43: 2Lt. HDB Snelgrove, 2AM W Addison (b-KIA)
9	21 Aug	DH.4 A7566	Near Ascq – RFC 55: 2Lt. CW Davyes (WIA/POW), 2Lt. JL Richardson (KIA)
10	17 Sep	DH.5 A9409	South of Izel[-lès-Équerchin] – RFC 41: 2Lt. Robert Edward Taylor (KIA)
11	24 Sep	Lattice-tail 2-seater	East of Loos – ?
12	28 Sep	Sopwith Camel B6209	West of Wingles – RFC 43: 2Lt. RP Hood (KIA)
13	" "	Sopwith Camel B2366 p.87	Near Vermelles – RFC 43: Capt. TS Wynn (OK)
14	18 Oct	SE.5a B528	Near Deûlémont – RFC 56: Lt. JD Gilbert (KIA)
15	28 Nov	DH.5	Near Poelcappelle – RFC 32: 2Lt. D Francis (WIA)
16	5 Dec	Sopwith Camel B2470	Near Westrozebeke – RFC 70: 2Lt. CGV Runnels-Moss (KIA)
17	6 Jan 1918	Nieuport 27 B6831	Near Bikschote – RFC 29: Capt. RH Rusby (WIA)
18	28 Jan	S.E.5	Northwest of Houthulst Forest – ?
19	29 Jan	Bristol F.2b	Near Zillebeke – ?
20	18 Feb	Sopwith Camel N6347	Near Zandvoorde – RNAS 10: FSLt. RE Burr (WIA/DOW)
21	27 Mar	RE.8 B6528?	Near Albert – RFC 42?: Lt. JVR Brown, 2Lt. CF Warren (b-WIA)?
22	28 Mar	Sopwith Camel C8224	Between Thiepval and Courcelette – RFC 43: 2Lt. Charles Roland Maasdorp (KIA)
23	6 Apr	Sopwith Camel C8247	Near Hamel – RAF 43: Lt. HS Lewis (KIA)
24	31 May	Breguet XIV	Southwest of Soissons – *Esc Br* 29: *Sous-Lt.* Charles Maurice Béranger, *Sgt.* Edouard Simon Wolf (b-KIA) OR *Sgt.* Hippolyte Julien Martin, *Sol.* Jean René Galbrun (b-KIA)
25	2 Jun	Breguet XIV	Northwest of Neuilly[-Saint-Front] – *Esc Br* 108: *Sgt.* Marcel Charles Ernest Commandeur, *Sgt.* Marcel Hedman (b-KIA)
26	5 Jun	SPAD VII 7216 OR 5603	South of Buzancy – *Esc Spa* 62: *Sgt.* André Bernard (POW) OR *Sous-Lt.* Charles Quette (KIA)
27	6 Jun	SPAD VII	South of Faverolles – *Esc Spa* 69: *Sgt.* Jean Pierre Louis Alfred Bouilliant (KIA)
28	7 Jun	SPAD VII	East of Villers-Cotterêts: *Esc Spa* 86: *Sgt.* Kobayashi Shukunosuke (KIA)
29	13 Jun	SPAD	Northwest of Faverolles – multiple candidates from *Esc Spa* 98, *Spa* 37, *Spa* 12; but possibly *Spa* 98: *Cpl.* Jacques Edmond Chapal OR *Brig.* François Aleppe
30	14 Jun	SPAD	North of Saint-Pierre-Aigle – ?
31	23 Jun	Breguet XIV	Near La Ferté-Milon – ?
32	" "	Breguet XIV	Near Crouy – *Esc Br* 216: *Lt.* Pierre François Hilaire Félicien Tournadre, *Sol.* Pic (b-KIA)
33	24 Jun	Salmson 2A2	Southeast of Montigny[-Lengrain] – *Esc Br* 35: *Cpt.* François Pierre Paul Fageol, *Lt.* Marie Daniel Eugène Faure (b-KIA)
34	25 Jun	SPAD XIII	Over Longpont Woods – *Esc Spa* 96: *Sgt.* William Vernon Booth, Jr. (WIA/DOW)

35 " "	SPAD VII	Ferme de Chavigny, Longpont – *Esc Spa 96: Cpl.* Edouard Aury (WIA)
36 30 Jun	SPAD XIII 8352? OR SPAD	near Faverolles – *Esc Spa 73 OR Spa 87?: Lt.* Bernard Charles Marie Alfred de Girval (KIA) OR *Sous-Lt.* Jean Onézime Lavergne (MIA/KIA)?
37 1 Jul	Breguet XIV 851	Near Villers-Cotterêts – *Esc Br 219: Lt.* Henri Dupont, *Sous-Lt.* Pierre André Joseph Schalbar (b-KIA)
38 " "	SPAD	East of Faverolles – ?
39 2 Jul	Nieuport 28 6347.3	Between Bézu-Saint-Germain – 27th Aero: 1Lt. Walter B Wanamaker (INJ/POW)
40 3 Jul	SPAD XIII	East of Laversine – *Esc Spa 65: Adj.* Georges Eugène Antoine Lienhard (KIA)
41 1 Aug	Nieuport 28 6275.17	North of Cramaille -- 27th Aero: 1Lt. Charles Bowcock Sands (KIA)
42 " "	Breguet XIV 2752	North of Muret-et-Crouttes – *Esc Spa 62: MdL.* André Gabriel Léopold LeBrun, *Lt.* Marie Robert Brumauld des Allées (b-KIA)
43 " "	SPAD	North of Beugneux – (multiple candidates)
44 4 Aug	SPAD XIII	South of Braine – *Esc Spa 76?: Sgt.* Gratien Auguste Henri Verrier (KIA)
45 8 Aug	SE.5a C1894	Near Fontaine-lès-Cappy – RAF 1: Lt. GR Touchstone (WIA/POW)
46 " "	SE.5a D6962	Southeast of Barleux – RAF 1: Capt. KC Mills (KIA)
47 " "	Sopwith Camel D9481	Southeast of Foucaucourt[-en-Santerre] – RAF 54: Lt. RE Taylor (POW)
48 9 Aug	Sopwith Camel D6520	South of Vauvillers – RAF 201: Lt. R Stone (KIA)
49 " "	Sopwith Camel D8161	Southeast of Herleville – RAF 65: 2Lt. AS Sinclair (POW)
50 10 Aug	Sopwith Camel B7399.Z	South of Morcourt – RAF 3: Lt. VB McIntosh (KIA)
51 " "	Sopwith Camel F5934	East of Fay – RAF 201: Lt. Charles Lewis Wood, Jr. (WIA/POW/DOW)
52 11 Aug	DH.9 D1721	Near Chaulnes – RAF 98: 2Lt. SD Connolly (POW), 2Lt. EH Clayton (WIA/POW/DOW)
53 12 Aug	SE.5a E3984	Near Péronne – RAF 40: Capt. IF Hind (KIA)
54 14 Aug	Bristol F.2b C852	Near Vermandovillers – RAF 88: Lt. AR Stedman, 2Lt. GR Howard (b-POW)
55 15 Aug	Sopwith Camel	Near Herleville – 148th Aero: 1Lt. Lawrence T. Wyly (WIA)
56 16 Aug	SPAD XIII 4848	South of Foucaucourt – *Esc Spa 3: Sous-Lt.* Jean Edouard Caël (POW)
57 21 Aug	SE.5a	South of Hébuterne – ?
58 " "	Sopwith Camel E1478?	Near Courcelles[-le-Comte] – 148th Pursuit?: 2Lt. TW Imes (WIA)?
59 22 Aug	Sopwith Camel F1969	North of Bray[-sur-Somme] – RAF 80: 2Lt. AL Tupman (KIA)
60 " "	SE.5a B8422.B	West of Maricourt – RAF 40: Capt. Tom F Hazell (OK)
61 26 Sep	DH.9	Near Montigny-lès-Metz – RAF 99 (multiple candidates)
62 " "	DH.9	South of Metz – RAF 99 (multiple candidates)

*pilot listed first

b-	both occupants		
DOI	died of injuries	KIA	killed in action
DOW	died of wounds	POW	prisoner of war
INJ	injured	WIA	wounded in action

Facing Page: Hans Bauer's portrait of Udet that was published on the cover of the German magazine *Jugend*.

JVGEND

1918 Nr. 48

Pour le Mérite Winners by Date of Award

Recipient	Date of Award
Hptm. Oswald Boelcke	January 12, 1916
Oblt. Max Immelmann	January 12, 1916
Oblt. Hans-Joachim Buddecke	April 14, 1916
Lt. Kurt Wintgens	July 1, 1916
Lt. Max *Ritter* von Mulzer	July 8, 1916
Lt. Otto Parschau	July 10, 1916
Lt. Walter Höhndorf	July 20, 1916
Oblt. Ernst *Freiherr* von Althaus	July 21, 1916
Lt. Wilhelm Frankl	August 12, 1916
Hptm. Rudolf Berthold	October 12, 1916
Lt. Gustav Leffers	November 5, 1916
Lt. Albert Dossenbach	November 11, 1916
Oblt. Hans Berr	December 4, 1916
Rittm. Manfred *Freiherr* von Richthofen	January 12, 1917
Genlt. Ernst von Hoeppner	April 8, 1917
Oberst Hermann von der Lieth-Thomsen	April 8, 1917
Lt. Werner Voss	April 8, 1917
Oblt. Fritz Otto Bernert	April 23, 1917
Lt. (Carl) Emil Schaefer	April 26, 1917
Oblt. Kurt Wolff	May 4, 1917
Lt. Heinrich Gontermann	May 14, 1917
Lt. Lothar *Freiherr* von Richthofen	May 14, 1917
Lt. Carl Allmenröder	June 14, 1917
Hptm. Ernst Brandenburg	June 14, 1917
Hptm. Paul *Freiherr* von Pechmann	July 31, 1917
Hptm. Adolf *Ritter* von Tutschek	August 3, 1917
Oblt. Eduard *Ritter* von Dostler	August 6, 1917
Fkpt. Peter Strasser	August 20, 1917
Lt. Max *Ritter* von Müller	September 3, 1917
Hptm. Rudolf Kleine	October 4, 1917
Lt. Walter von Bülow-Bothkamp	October 8, 1917
Lt. Curt Wüsthoff	November 22, 1917
Lt. Erwin Böhme	November 24, 1917
Lt. Julius Buckler	December 4, 1917
Lt. Hans Klein	December 4, 1917
Hptm. Eduard *Ritter* von Schleich	December 4, 1917
Hptm. Alfred Keller	December 4, 1917
Kptlt. Friedrich Christiansen	December 11, 1917
Lt. Heinrich Bongartz	December 23, 1917
Oblt. Hermann Fricke	December 23, 1917
Oblt. Hans-Georg Horn	December 23, 1917

Recipient	Date of Award
Hptm. Bruno Loerzer	February 12, 1918
Lt. Heinrich Kroll	March 29, 1918
Kptlt. Horst *Freiherr* Treusch von Buttlar-Brandenfels	April 9, 1918
Oblt. Ernst Udet	April 9, 1918
Lt. Carl Menckhoff	April 23, 1918
Hptm. Hermann Köhl	May 21, 1918
Oblt. Erich Loewenhardt	May 31, 1918
Lt. Fritz Pütter	May 31, 1918
Oblt. Hermann Göring	June 2, 1918
Lt. Friedrich Nielebock	June 2, 1918
Lt. Rudolf Windisch	June 6, 1918
Lt. Wilhelm Paul Schreiber	June 8, 1918
Lt. Hans Kirschstein	June 24, 1918
Oblt. Otto Kissenberth	June 30, 1918
Lt. Emil Thuy	June 30, 1918
Lt. Peter Rieper	July 7, 1918
Lt. Fritz Rumey	July 10, 1918
Lt. Josef Jacobs	July 18, 1918
Lt. zur See Gotthard Sachsenberg	August 5, 1918
Hptm. Franz Walz	August 9, 1918
Lt. Josef Veltjens	August 16, 1918
Lt. Karl Bolle	August 28, 1918
Lt. Theo Osterkamp	September 2, 1918
Oblt. Fritz *Ritter* von Röth	September 8, 1918
Lt. Otto Könnecke	September 26, 1918
Lt. Walter Blume	September 30, 1918
Lt. Wilhelm Griebsch	September 30, 1918
Hptm. Leo Leonhardy	October 2, 1918
Oblt. Robert *Ritter* von Greim	October 8, 1918
Oblt. Jürgen von Grone	October 13, 1918
Oblt. Erich Homburg	October 13, 1918
Oblt. Albert Müller-Kahle	October 13, 1918
Oblt. Oskar *Freiherr* von Boenigk	October 25, 1918
Lt. Franz Büchner	October 25, 1918
Lt. Arthur Laumann	October 25, 1918
Lt. Olivier *Freiherr* von Beaulieu Marconnay	October 26, 1918
Lt. Karl Thom	November 1, 1918
Lt. Paul Bäumer	November 2, 1918
Lt. Ulrich Neckel	November 8, 1918
Lt. Carl Degelow	November 9, 1918

Pour le Mérite Winners Alphabetically

Recipient	Date of Award	Recipient	Date of Award
Lt. Carl Allmenröder	June 14, 1917	*Hptm.* Rudolf Kleine	October 4, 1917
Oblt. Ernst *Freiherr* von Althaus	July 21, 1916	*Hptm.* Hermann Köhl	May 21, 1918
Lt. Paul Bäumer	November 2, 1918	*Lt.* Otto Könnecke	September 26, 1918
Lt. Olivier *Freiherr* von Beaulieu Marconnay	October 26, 1918	*Lt.* Heinrich Kroll	March 29, 1918
		Lt. Arthur Laumann	October 25, 1918
Oblt. Fritz Otto Bernert	April 23, 1917	*Lt.* Gustav Leffers	November 5, 1916
Oblt. Hans Berr	December 4, 1916	*Hptm.* Leo Leonhardy	October 2, 1918
Hptm. Rudolf Berthold	October 12, 1916	*Oberst* Hermann von der Lieth-Thomsen	April 8, 1917
Lt. Walter Blume	September 30, 1918	*Hptm.* Bruno Loerzer	February 12, 1918
Lt. Erwin Böhme	November 24, 1917	*Oblt.* Erich Loewenhardt	May 31, 1918
Hptm. Oswald Boelcke	January 12, 1916	*Lt.* Carl Menckhoff	April 23, 1918
Oblt. Oskar *Freiherr* von Boenigk	October 25, 1918	*Lt.* Max *Ritter* von Müller	September 3, 1917
Lt. Karl Bolle	August 28, 1918	*Oblt.* Albert Müller-Kahle	October 13, 1918
Lt. Heinrich Bongartz	December 23, 1917	*Lt.* Max *Ritter* von Mulzer	July 8, 1916
Hptm. Ernst Brandenburg	June 14, 1917	*Lt.* Ulrich Neckel	November 8, 1918
Lt. Julius Buckler	December 4, 1917	*Lt.* Friedrich Nielebock	June 2, 1918
Oblt. Hans-Joachim Buddecke	April 14, 1916	*Lt.* Theo Osterkamp	September 2, 1918
Lt. Franz Büchner	October 25, 1918	*Lt.* Otto Parschau	July 10, 1916
Lt. Walter von Bülow-Bothkamp	October 8, 1917	*Hptm.* Paul *Freiherr* von Pechmann	July 31, 1917
Kptlt. Horst *Freiherr* Treusch von Buttlar-Brandenfels	April 9, 1918	*Lt.* Fritz Pütter	May 31, 1918
		Lt. Lothar *Freiherr* von Richthofen	May 14, 1917
Kptlt. Friedrich Christiansen	December 11, 1917	*Rittm.* Manfred *Freiherr* von Richthofen	January 12, 1917
Lt. Carl Degelow	November 9, 1918		
Lt. Albert Dossenbach	November 11, 1916	*Lt.* Peter Rieper	July 7, 1918
Oblt. Eduard *Ritter* von Dostler	August 6, 1917	*Oblt.* Fritz *Ritter* von Röth	September 8, 1918
Lt. Wilhelm Frankl	August 12, 1916	*Lt.* Fritz Rumey	July 10, 1918
Oblt. Hermann Fricke	December 23, 1917	*Lt. zur See* Gotthard Sachsenberg	August 5, 1918
Oblt. Hermann Göring	June 2, 1918	*Lt.* (Carl) Emil Schaefer	April 26, 1917
Lt. Heinrich Gontermann	May 14, 1917	*Hptm.* Eduard *Ritter* von Schleich	December 4, 1917
Oblt. Robert *Ritter* von Greim	October 8, 1918	*Lt.* Wilhelm Paul Schreiber	June 8, 1918
Lt. Wilhelm Griebsch	September 30, 1918	*Fkpt.* Peter Strasser	August 20, 1917
Oblt. Jürgen von Grone	October 13, 1918	*Lt.* Karl Thom	November 1, 1918
Lt. Walter Höhndorf	July 20, 1916	*Lt.* Emil Thuy	June 30, 1918
Genlt. Ernst von Hoeppner	April 8, 1917	*Hptm.* Adolf *Ritter* von Tutschek	August 3, 1917
Oblt. Erich Homburg	October 13, 1918	*Oblt.* Ernst Udet	April 9, 1918
Oblt. Hans-Georg Horn	December 23, 1917	*Lt.* Josef Veltjens	August 16, 1918
Oblt. Max Immelmann	January 12, 1916	*Lt.* Werner Voss	April 8, 1917
Lt. Josef Jacobs	July 18, 1918	*Hptm.* Franz Walz	August 9, 1918
Hptm. Alfred Keller	December 4, 1917	*Lt.* Rudolf Windisch	June 6, 1918
Lt. Hans Kirschstein	June 24, 1918	*Lt.* Kurt Wintgens	July 1, 1916
Oblt. Otto Kissenberth	June 30, 1918	*Oblt.* Kurt Wolff	May 4, 1917
Lt. Hans Klein	December 4, 1917	*Lt.* Curt Wüsthoff	November 22, 1917

Index

Appendix

The Controversial Markings of Udet's *Du doch nicht!!"* Fokker D.VII

By Greg VanWyngarden and Lance Bronnenkant, PhD.
"But I thought the stripes on the top wing were red and white? That's the way it is in all the pictures!" No doubt, this may be the initial reaction of many readers when they see profile number 16 – Udet's classic, iconic Fokker D.VII (OAW) with the defiant legend on the elevator and the dazzling stripes on the wing. Illustrations, models and even full-size flying replicas of this aircraft with *red* and white stripes are ubiquitous in the community of WWI aviation enthusiasts and their literature. The depictions of this short-lived D.VII have changed a number of times over the past 60 years; we felt that the reasons for our particular interpretation, and the history behind the shifting versions, should be explained in this appendix. We are certain that many readers will still prefer their own differing interpretations, which is certainly their prerogative.

Let us re-emphasize that there is only one good photo of this iconic Fokker known to us today (originally published as a halftone in the original edition of *Mein Fliegerleben*), and even that photo is a problematic one. There are no contemporary descriptions or surviving combat reports that would reveal its colors, unlike D.VIIF 4235/18 and Albatros D.V 4476/17. Furthermore, gleaning information from that single photo is a hazardous enterprise for two reasons. Udet posed directly in front of the rudder, obscuring most of the aircraft; in this photo we have no view of the machine's fuselage, only the tailplane, elevator and a glimpse of the wings. The other problem is, this photo was highly retouched for publication, as were all of the other photos in the book. The anonymous retouching artist did not know much about aircraft, (as demonstrated in the photo of Bolle's D.VII of *Jasta* Boelcke which appears in the photo section between pp.96 and 97, captioned

'Bodenschatz, Udet, Bolle'. The bright white stripes on the upper wing of *Du doch nicht!!* were distinctly highlighted, and the aileron demarcation line has disappeared, visible only in the dark stripe that touches the starboard wing cross; there is no sign of the starboard aileron control horn either. In fact, as Fokker D.VII specialist Jörn Leckscheid points out "No wing rib details of any form can be made out on the upper wing at all, and these were very prominent on the D.VII." The interplane and center section struts were drawn in to emphasize them, and the streamers trailing from the elevator were also enhanced. We may never know how accurately the artist portrayed the appearance and number of those intriguing top wing stripes; the white stripes appear slightly wider than the dark ones, but again this is likely due to the retoucher. Some enthusiasts looked at the small portion of the cross visible on the starboard wing and held that there were no white outlines on the cross. This would, some would say, indicate that the wing stripes must have been red/white and not black/white, as black un-outlined crosses would not stand out against the black stripes. However, close examination of the photo does discover (in the authors' opinion) a narrow white border on the inboard edge of the lower cross arm. This border was subdued and almost lost in the printing process – but it was there.

To our knowledge, the first attempt to portray the famous striped-wing Fokker of Udet in color was made by artist Merv Corning, for a print published in 1961. Corning created a highly-regarded series of aviation history paintings that were issued as prints in the Leach Corporation's "Heritage of the Air" collection. For their day these paintings were well-researched (something new in aviation art) and many of his WWI scenes are still well regarded and collectable. Corning illustrated the famous event of 29 June 1918 when Udet was shot down in *Du doch nicht!!* in his attack on a French Breguet, and titled

Above: A close inspection of the highly-edited photo of *Du doch nicht!!* shows clear signs of a border along the upper wing's *Balkenkreuz* insignia.

it *Fall of the Flying Fool*. Corning had obviously read Udet's own account of this harrowing combat in the British translation of *Mein Fliegerleben* (published with only one post-war photo in 1937 as *Ace of the Black Cross*). The artist must have also acquired an original copy of *Mein Fliegerleben*, which included the now-famous photo as well as Udet's combat report for 26 September, describing 4253/18 as having a red fuselage with the letters "LO". He had also seen the now-familiar photo, labeled in this volume as U90, showing Udet with 4253/18 at Fürth which gave a hint of the "LO!" emblem.

Corning combined these elements into a striking image of what he felt Udet's *Du doch nicht!!* D.VII would have looked like. The Fokker was shown with the cowling panels of a late Fokker-built D.VII and a small cross confined to the rudder (which we now know was characteristic only of late OAW machines), with a bright red fuselage and tail. He portrayed about 36 stripes on the top wing; since he knew that Udet's later Fokker had a red fuselage, he understandably assumed that the stripes on the top wing were red and white like a barber pole; it looked great, and thus an iconic legend was born. Corning's portrayal of the white chevron markings on the tail stopped at the leading edges of the horizontal stabilizer and did not extend to the apex or point of a typical chevron (this portion of the chevron is not visible in the photo, obscured by Udet). Corning's well-distributed print set the pattern for every depiction of Udet's Fokker that followed. Later in 1961, Fawcett Publications issued their popular paperback *Sky Fighters of World War I*, an anthology of pilot biographies. The cover painting by aviation artist Jo Kotula depicted Udet's Fokker in action against a Spad, and Kotula followed Corning's depiction in nearly every aspect – thus publicizing the candy striped D.VII even more. Shortly after, an original, flyable Fokker D.VII (with a replacement

Hispano-Suiza engine) owned by the movie stunt pilots Paul Mantz and Frank Tallman was repainted in an approximation of the "Udet" markings. Photos of this unique flying Fokker appeared in many magazines and in airshows and TV programs of the era. Plastic model companies issued kits with box art for this version. In 1970 the new American translation of *Mein Fliegerleben* appeared as *Ace of the Iron Cross* and both the hardback and paperback versions naturally featured dynamic illustrations of the red/white striped machine on their covers. In fact, in author VanWyngarden's monograph *Von Richthofen's Flying Circus*, published by Albatros Productions Ltd. in 1995, the accepted version of this machine as an early Fokker-built variant with red/white stripes was depicted on the front cover – which reflected the author's limited knowledge and resources at the time.

As stated in the commentary for profile 16, Werner Preuss' statement of 3 July – that he saw a red Fokker and immediately recognized it as Udet – indicates that Udet was already well-known for flying a crimson D.VII and thus *Du doch nicht!!* most likely had a red fuselage.

Some new interpretations came to light in the Winter 1988 issue of *Windsock International*, a magazine catering to WWI modelers. Dan-San Abbott's article *Udet's Fokker D.VII Fighters* presented his own revisionist version of *Du doch nicht!!*, with his three-view drawing and Ray Rimell's accompanying color profile on the rear cover. Dan focused on what appears to be a longitudinal white 'strip' or rectangular shape that seems to appear in the crook of Udet's right arm in the famous photo. Dan interpreted this as a portion of a wide white stripe that he thought extended from the leading tip of the chevron on the tail on top of the fuselage, and illustrated this as two white stripes marked on the fuselage deck from tail to cockpit. This new interpretation with the broad white stripes on the fuselage decking became the basis for more models and paintings, and remains popular.

This ever-popular D.VII came under further examination and revision in Albatros Production's *Fokker D.VII Anthology 2*, in 1999. In that volume, British Fokker historian Dave Roberts presented his own revelations in his article *The Importance of Being Erni's*. He relayed some opinions from the late A.E. "Ed" Ferko, a respected historian of German WWI aviation (Ed had also spoken of this topic to Greg VanWyngarden). In disputing the 'white stripe on top of the fuselage' version, Ed Ferko wrote: "*If you take a moment to try to lay out the fuselage contour it is almost impossible to have a white bar so far to the side of where the fuselage should be –*

actually Udet has a book under one arm! Moreover, that white thing between arm and body has a radius which makes it impossible to be a white stripe or bar." Dave Roberts agreed with Ed's view, stating that, *"...the top of the line is indeed too far left to be the on the fuselage...Apart from Ed's book theory, the other possibility is clumsy retouching for publication in* Mein Fliegerleben.*"* Dave further opined that this was an early OAW-built D.VII, based on other photos of early *Jasta* 4 Fokkers and the light-colored rib tapes seen on the lower wing – and we agree with this conclusion. He also depicted the chevron on the tailplane just as we have depicted it in profile 16, based on the photos of similar chevron markings on Udet's OAW-built D.VII (profile 17) and Dr.I 593/17. Dave's examination of the photo indicated that there were 33 stripes, *"including fragments on the balance of the port aileron and leading corner."* He chose to portray the nose in *Jasta* 4's black unit marking color, as we have.

Dave also mentioned a little-known piece of evidence that he had discussed with VanWyngarden and others, but which remains unknown to most enthusiasts. In the 1935 film *Wunder des Fliegens* (starring Udet) we get a fascinating glimpse of Udet's Berlin apartment and the walls of his study where many of his wartime trophies were displayed. As the camera pans across the wall, we see – next to a large portrait of Boelcke – a frustratingly small view of a framed triptych of photos which have never been seen elsewhere. Even in these tiny blurry images, we can see the one on the right is a view of a D.VII with a striped top wing and part of a "LO!" emblem. It must be an otherwise unknown photo of *Du doch nicht!!* Though it does not reveal much, it does show that there were no white stripes on top of the dark-painted fuselage. Thus, we omitted such stripes from profile 16.

As for our opinion that the dark stripes were black and not red, this has been partially explained in the commentary for profile 16. Udet's previous experience with the black and white 'optical illusion' Dr.I 586/17 is no doubt what influenced him to have similar disruptive stripes applied to the top wing of his new D.VII. There was considerable experimentation being carried out with such striping, especially in *Jasta* 6 by Kirchstein and later by Ulrich Neckel. The striping on these aircraft, and in other units, is believed to have consistently been black and white. Udet probably rarely flew in the same formation as Kirchstein's *Jasta* 6 Fokker D.VII, and Udet's red fuselage would provide ample distinction from the black/white striped fuselage and tail of Kirchstein's machine if they were ever seen together. Author VanWyngarden discussed this

Above: An image of Udet's study from the movie *Wunder des Fliegens*. The triptych at upper left contains a photo (far right) of a Fokker D.VII with a striped upper wing and Udet's "LO!" insignia. As far as we know, this could only have been *Du doch nicht!!*

issue with the renowned historian Alex Imrie in telephone conversations. Alex had interviewed many *JG* I veterans and knew Udet's mechanic Walter Behrend. Alex was certain that the stripes were black and white. For this reason, it was illustrated with black/white stripes in Osprey's *Aircraft of the Aces 53:Fokker D VII Aces of World War 1, Part 1*, co-authored by VanWyngarden and Norman Franks in 2003.

Further confirmation of the black/white thesis has kindly been supplied by the authors' colleague, German historian Bruno Schmäling, who writes:

"When I visited Alex Imrie the first time in 1977, he showed me a color painting, done by an artist for him, [of] Udet's Fokker D.VII "Du doch nicht!" The stripes on the upper wing were black and white! The fuselage was red. I was very surprised, as I believed at this time, like many others the stripes were red and white. Alex told me that his information from Jasta *4 pilots was, that the stripes are black and white. He said the information he got from* Jasta *4 pilots [was] that Udet adopted the black and white striped upper wing from the Triplane (from Kirchstein) to [apply to] one of his Fokker D.VIIs. Alex convinced me that the upper wing was striped black and white....I spoke with* Jasta *4 pilots, especially Richard Kraut; I told him about Alex's information, and he confirmed it, as "black and white" were the colors of* Jagdstaffel *4. I personally am convinced that the upper wing was black and white striped and NOT red and white."*

Our interpretation that *Du doch nicht!!* had a black nose and that his later red D.VIIs did not, is largely a subjective opinion. In his article *Meine Ehrfahrung mit dem BMW Motor, Typ IIIa*, Udet wrote that with his BMW Fokker he quickly left his "loyal black-nosed [Mercedes] Fokker *Staffel* behind and below..." While it is true that most *Jasta* 4 D.VIIs had black noses, wheels and struts, Udet may have opted for largely red coloration on his BMW D.VIIs which would make it easy for his *Staffel* to identify him and to facilitate confirmation of his victories. His combat reports for 8 August and 26 September both mention only a "red fuselage" and nothing about a black nose. The statements of his pilots, and by Wanamaker and Caël who were attacked by Udet, describe only a "red Fokker". As always, the reader is left to arrive at their own conclusions about this and other details of Udet's machines, based on the evidence we have presented.

The authors express their gratitude to Jörn Lecksheid and Bruno Schmäling for their valued generosity and input. The conclusions presented here are the sole responsibility of the authors. Perhaps someday, additional photos may come to light in some German archive that will provide more conclusive evidence.

Ernst Udet has long been an object of great appeal to aviation enthusiasts and the interest in, and arguments over, minutiae of his aircraft will no doubt continue. Udet was a fascinating character, and even his former enemies came to admire him in the post-war years. We will leave the last word to the French aeronautical journalist Jacques Mortane. Normally no friend of Germans, the fiercely patriotic writer interviewed Udet in 1926 and wrote: *"Udet, ace of aces of the German Air Force...was always a loyal and chivalrous opponent. The French airmen whom he shot down and who were taken prisoner, all agree in declaring that their conqueror behaved towards them as a gentleman: he went to see them, bringing them candies, tobacco, and asking for letters for their parents that he was responsible for launching from his aircraft at high altitude over our lines. He defended his flag: it was his duty."*

Left: An early portrait of Udet. (photo courtesy of Greg VanWyngarden)

Facing Page: The cover of *Hals und Beinbruch*, Udet's published collection of caricatures and sketches. (photo courtesy of Greg VanWyngarden)

Glossary

Adjudant	Warrant Officer
Armee	Army
Armee-Abteilung (AA)	Army unit
Armee-Flug-Park (AFP)	Army aviation supply depot
Artillerie Flieger-Abteilung (AFA)	Artillery cooperation aviation unit
Brigadier (Brig.)	Corporal (cavalry or artillery)
Capitaine (Capt.)	Captain
Chef des Feldflugwesens (Feldflugchef)	Chief of Army Field Aviation
Caporal (Cpl.)	Corporal
CO	Commanding officer
Compagnie d'aérostieres (C d'a)	Aeronaut (balloon) company
der Reserve (d.R.)	of the Reserves
Doktoringenieur (Dr.Ing.)	Doctor of Engineering
Ehrenbecher	Honor goblet
Eindecker	Monoplane
Escadrille (Esc.)	Aviation unit
Fähnrich	Senior Officer Candidate
Fahnenjunker	Junior Officer Candidate
Feldflieger-Abteilung (FFA)	Field aviation unit
Feldflugchef	Chief of Army Field Aviation
Feldwebel	Sergeant
Flieger-Abteilung (FA)	Aviation unit
Feldwebelleutnant	Sergeant Major Lieutenant (U.S. Warrant Officer)
Flieger-Abteilung Artillerie (FA(A))	Artillery cooperation aviation unit
Flieger-Ersatz-Abteilung (FEA)	Aviation replacement unit
Fliegerleutnant	Aviation 2nd Lieutenant
Fliegerschule	Aviation school
Fliegertruppe	Air Service
Freiherr	"Free lord" title of nobility
Führer	Leader
Gefreiter (Gefr.)	Private 1st Class
General (Gen.)	General
Generalleutnant (GenLt.)	Lieutenant General (U.S. Major General)
Generalmajor (GenMaj.)	Major General (U.S. Brigadier General)
Generaloberst	Colonel General (U.S. Four-Star General)
Geschwader	Squadron or formation
Geschwaderführer	CO of a *Geschwader*
Graf	Count
Hauptmann (Hptm.)	Captain
Heeresbericht	Army reports
Herr	Mister
Inspektion der Fliegertruppe (Idflieg)	Inspectorate of Army Flying Troops or Air Service
Jagdgeschwader (JG)	Squadron consisting of several *Jagdstaffeln*
Jagdstaffel (Jasta)	Fighter unit
Jastaschule	Fighter pilot training school
Kampfeinsitzer-Kommando (KEK)	Single-seat fighter unit
Kampfstaffel (Kasta)	Combat unit
Kampfgeschwader der Obersten Heeresleitung (Kagohl/KG)	Supreme Command Combat Squadron
Kogenluft	Commanding General of the Army Air Service or his staff
Kommandeur der Flieger (Kofl.)	Officer/staff in charge of aviation for an army
Kriegsschule	War school

Kriegstagebuch	War diary
Kuk Luftfahrtruppen	Austro-Hungarian Aviation Troops or Air Service
Leutnant (Lt.)	2nd Lieutenant
Luftstreitkräfte	Air force
Major	Major
Maréchal des Logis (MdL.)	Sergeant (cavalry or artillery)
Militär-Flieger-Schule	Military aviation school
Mitrailleur	Machine gunner
Nachrichtenblatt der Luftstreitkräfte	Air Force news publication
Oberleutnant (Oblt.)	1st Lieutenant
Oberste Heeresleitung	Supreme Command
Oberstleutnant (Oberstlt.)	Lieutenant Colonel
Offizier-Stellvertreter (Offz-Stv.)	Warrant Officer
Ordenskissen	Funeral cushion with decorations
RAF	Royal Air Force
RFC	Royal Flying Corps
Ritter	Knight (honorary title)
Rittmeister (Rittm.)	Cavalry Captain
RNAS	Royal Naval Air Service
Schutzstaffel (Schusta)	Protection unit
Sergeant (Sgt.)	Sergeant
Soldat	Private
Sonderstaffel	Special unit
Stabsoffizier der Flieger (Stofl.)	Aviation officer/staff for an army
Staffel	Unit
Staffelführer	Commanding officer of a *Staffel*
Unteroffizier (Uffz.)	Corporal
Versuchs- und Übungsflugpark	Aviation depot for testing and training
Vizefeldwebel (Vzfw.)	Vice Sergeant or Vice Sergeant Major
Werkmeister	Mechanics Foreman

Right: A candid snapshot of Udet.

Bibliography

Books

Bailey, Frank and Christophe Cony. *The French Air Service War Chronology 1914–1918* (London: Grub Street, 2001)

Binot, Jean-Marc. *Georges Guynemer* (Paris: Fayard, 2017)

Bodenschatz, Karl. *Jagd in Flanderns Himmel* (Munich: Verlag Knorr & Hirth, 1935)

Bronnenkant, Lance. *The Imperial German Eagles in World War I: Their Postcards and Pictures*, Vol.1 (Atglen: Schiffer Publishing, 2006)

Buckler, Julius. Malaula! *Der Kampfruf meiner Staffel* (Berlin: Steiniger-Verlage,1939)

DeWolfe Howe, M.A. *Memoirs of the Harvard Dead in the War Against Germany* (Cambridge: Harvard Univ. Press, 1920)

Franks, Norman, Frank Bailey and Rick Duiven. *The Jasta Pilots* (London: Grub Street, 1996)

Franks, Norman, Frank Bailey and Rick Duiven. *The Jasta War Chronology* (London: Grub Street, 1998)

Grosz, Peter. *Fokker Fighters D.I–IV* (Berkhamsted: Albatros Productions, 1999)

Grosz, Peter. *Pfalz E.I–E.VI* (Berkhamsted: Albatros Productions, 1996)

Henshaw, Trevor. *The Sky Their Battlefield* II (London: Fetubi Books, 2014)

Herris, Jack. *Albatros Aircraft of WWI*, Vol.4 (Aeronaut Books, 2017)

Herris, Jack. *Aviatik Aircraft of WWI* (Aeronaut Books, 2014)

Herris, Jack. *Germany's Fighter Competitions of 1918* (Aeronaut Books, 2013)

Imrie, Alex. *German Fighter Units 1914–May 1917* (Botley: Osprey, 1978)

Ishoven, Armand van. *Ernst Udet* (Wien: Paul Neff Verlag, 1977)

Ishoven, Armand van. *The Fall of an Eagle: The Life of Fighter Ace Ernst Udet* (London: William Kimber, 1979)

Kilduff, Peter. *The Red Baron Combat Wing* (London: Arms & Armour, 1998)

Leaman, Paul. *The Fokker Triplane* (Hersham: Chevron Publishing, 2003)

Loeff, Wolfgang. *Propeller überm Feind* (Köln: Hermann Schaffstein, 1934)

Mahncke, Alfred. *For Kaiser and Hitler* (Pulborough: Tattered Flag, 2011)

Monkhouse, George. *Mercedes Benz: Grand Prix Racing 1934–1955* (London: New Cavendish Books, 1984)

Müller, Leonhard. *Fliegerleutnant Heinrich Gontermann* (?: Verlag des Westdeutsches Jünglingsbunde, ?)

O'Connor, Neal. *Aviation Awards of Imperial Germany in World War I and the Men Who earned Them*, Vol.4 (Princeton: Foundation for Aviation World War I, 1995)

Schmäling, Bruno and Winfried Bock, *Royal Prussian Jagdstaffel 30* (Aeronaut Books, 2014)

Udet, Ernst. *Ace of the Black Cross* (London: Newnes, 1937)

Udet, Ernst. *Ace of the Iron Cross* (Garden City: Doubleday, 1970)

Udet, Ernst. *Kreuz wider Kokarde* (Berlin: Gustav Braunbeck, 1918)

Udet, Ernst. *Mein Fliegerleben* (Berlin: Deutscher Verlag, 1935)

VanWyngarden, Greg. *Albatros Aces of World War 1*, Part 2 (Botley: Osprey, 2007)

Wenzl, Richard. *Richthofen-Flieger* (Karlsruhe: Badische Zeitung, 1918)

Periodicals & Newspapers

Cross & Cockade (U.S.)
2:2 (1961) "My Experiences with the B.M.W. Motor Type IIIa" trans. by Alex Imrie
3:4 (1962) "Die Gebrüder Gabriel (The Gabriel Brothers" by Alex Imrie
5:4 (1964) "The Two Faces of Chivalry in the Air War" by George Shiras
7:4 (1966) "Jagdflieger Friedrich Noltenius" by A.E. Ferko

Das Propellerblatt
12 (2005) "Vizefeldwebel Gustav Bauer – Frontflieger, Fluglehrer, Erprobungsflieger" by Reinhard Kastner and Reinhard Zankl

Fawcett Battle Stories
(May 1931) "How I Shot Down 62 Planes – From the War Log of Ernst Udet" by David B. Rogers

La Vie Aérienne
(5 February 1920) "Le Lieutenant Udet Nous Écrit…" by Jacques Mortane
(5 February 1920) "Mes Débuts D'Aviateur" by Ernst Udet

Motor (May-June 1919) "Meine Erfahrung mit dem BMW-Motor, Type IIIa" by Ernst Udet

Over the Front
18:3 (2003) "Udet's 10th: 2/Lt. Robert Edward Taylor, 41 Squadron, RFC" by Stewart Taylor
19:2 (2004) "Ten Days: Lt. Charles B. Sands, 27th AeroSquadron" by Stephen Lucas and Alan Toelle
28:2 (2013) "From the Pulpit to the Cockpit – Lt. Charles L. Wood, Jr., RAF" by Peter Kilduff
29:3 (2014) "Udet and the French 'Ace'" by Werner Preuss

Popular Aviation
(November 1931) "Former Enemies Now Friends"